THE ULTIMATE SPEAKERS' HANDBOOK

The Ultimate Speakers' Handbook

More than 500 Stories for All Occasions

COMPILED BY ROBERT BACKHOUSE

Marshall Pickering
An Imprint of HarperCollins*Publishers*

Marshall Pickering is an Imprint of
HarperCollins*Religious*
Part of HarperCollins*Publishers*
77–85 Fulham Palace Road, London W6 8JB

First published in Great Britain in 1997
by Marshall Pickering

Copyright in this compilation and in the introduction © 1997 Robert Backhouse

1 3 5 7 9 10 8 6 4 2

A catalogue record for this book is
available from the British Library

0 551 03128X

Printed and bound in Great Britain by
Creative Print and Design (Wales), Ebbw Vale

Contents

Abortion 1
Abstinence 1
Achievement 1
Action (*see also* Faith) 1
Adoration of God 2
Adultery 2
Advice 3
Ambition
    (*see also* Contentment) 3
Angels 4
Anger 4
Anglicanism 5
Animals 4
Anxiety: *see* Worry 5
Apostles 5
Arguments 6
Arminianism 6
Assurance 6
Atheism 7

Backsliding 9
Baptism 9
Beauty 9
Becoming a Christian:
    see Conversion 10
Behaviour 10
Belief 10
Bereavement
    (*see also* Death; Dying) 11
Bible (see also Job, book of) 11
  Christ in the Bible 11
  The influence of the Bible 12
  Opposition to the Bible 14
  Bible reading 15
Birthdays 16
Bishops 16
Blindness (*see also* Endurance;
    Suffering) 17
  Spiritual blindness 17

Body *see* Newspapers 124
Brotherhood 17
Bulimia 17
Busybodies (*see also* Gossip) 18

Calling (*see also* Mission) 19
Challenge 19
Chance 19
Character 19
Children (*see also* Discipline;
    Family life) 20
Christ: *see* Jesus Christ 22
Christianity 22
Christlikeness 22
Church 23
Comfort 24
Contentment 24
Conversion (*see also*
    Repentance) 25
  Kriss Akabusi 28
  Augustine 29
  William Carey 30
  Sir William Dobbie 30
  James Fox 31
  Mitsuo Fuchida 32
  William Haslam 33
  Glenn Hoddle 33
  Jerome 34
  C. S. Lewis 34
  Martin Luther 35
  Steve Mc Queen 35
  Hugh Montefiore 36
  George Müller 36
  John Newton 37
  John Owen 38
  Joshua Poole 39
  Charles Simeon 39
  Charles Spurgeon 40
  Leo Tolstoy 41

Augustus Toplady 42
Jim Vaus 42
Counselling 42
Courage (*see also* Fear) 43
Covetousness 43
Creation 43
Criticism 43
Cross of Jesus (*see also* Gardens;
    Heresy; Ransom; Redemption;
    Success; Trees) 44
Cruelty (*see also* Refugees) 45
Cults 45

Death (*see also* Dying;
    Funerals) 47
Dedication (*see also* Work) 48
Demon possession 48
Depression 49
Disability and handicap 50
Discipleship (*see also*
    Martyrdom) 51
Discipline (*see also* Children) 54
Discoveries (*see also* Science) 54
Doubt 55
Dreams 55
Duty 55
Dying (*see also* Death;
    Funerals) 56

Education 58
Endurance 58
Equality (*see also* Inequality) 58
Eternal life 58
Eternity 58
Evangelism (*see also*
    Conversion) 59
Evil (*see also* Temptation) 62
Example 62
Experiences of God (*see also*
    Conversion) 63
    Thomas Aquinas 63
    Jonathan Edwards 63
    Jonathan Edwards' wife 63

D. L. Moody 64
David Brainerd 65

Faith (*see also* Action; Science;
    Work) 66
Faithfulness 67
Family life (*see also* Children) 67
Fashion 68
Fasting 68
Fear (*see also* Courage) 68
Fellowship 69
Film stars: *see* Hollywood; Success;
    Tears 69
Flattery 69
Forgiveness (*see also* Torture) 70
Free will 72
Freedom 73
Friendship 73
Funerals 74

Gardens 75
Generosity 75
Gentleness 75
Giving to God 75
God (*see also* Adoration of God;
    Atheism; Belief; Experiences of
    God; Giving to God; Peace;
    Power; Providence; Trinity;
    Trusting in God) 77
    Dedication to God 77
    The peace of God 77
    The presence of God 78
    Serving God / Christ 78
    The will of God 80
Gossip (*see also* Busybodies) 80
Grace 80
Grandmothers 82
Greed (*see also* Money;
    Possessions) 82
Growth 83

Habits 84
Healing (*see also* Dying) 84

Heaven (*see also* Eternity) 86
Heresy 86
Holiness 87
Hollywood 87
Holy Spirit (*see also* Experiences of
    God; Miracles) 87
Hope 89
Hospitality 89
Humankind 89
Humility 89
Husbands (*see also* Marriage) 91
Hypocrisy 91

Illness (*see also* Suffering) 93
Imprisonment (*see also* Suffering;
    Torture) 93
Incarnation (*see also* Jesus Christ) 93
Indecision 93
Indifference 94
Inequality (*see also* Equality) 94
Infallibility 94

Jesus: *see* Jesus Christ 95
Jesus Christ (*see also* Bible: Jesus in
    the Bible; Cross of Jesus;
    Humility; Incarnation) 95
  Jesus' historicity 95
  Jesus' person 96
  Jesus praying for us 97
  Jesus our righteousness 97
  Jesus our sacrifice 97
  Jesus' second coming 99
  Jesus our sin-bearer 100
  Jesus the way to God 100
Jews and Christians 100
Job, book of 100

Kindness 101
Kingdom of God 101
Knowledge 101

Lord's Supper 102
Love 103

Marriage (*see also* Husbands) 104
Martyrdom (*see also* Discipleship;
    Mission: Jim Elliot;
    Persecution; Prophetic
    messages; Suffering) 104
  Blind Chang 104
  John Huss 105
  Polycarp 108
  Ridley and Latimer 109
  William Tyndale 115
Miracles (*see also* Incarnation) 117
Mission (*see also* Angels; Calling;
    Patience; Protection) 118
  Jim Elliot 118
Money (*see also* Greed;
    Possessions) 120
Mothers 120
Music 121

Neighbours 123
News 123
Newspapers 124

Paganism 125
Patience 126
Peace: *see* God: Peace of God;
    Presence of God 126
People 126
Persecution (*see also* Martyrdom;
    Suffering) 126
Perseverance 128
Philosophy 129
Planning 130
Politeness 130
Politics 130
Possessions (*see also* Greed;
    Money) 130
Poverty (*see also* Money; Social
    action) 130
Power 131
Prayer 131
Preaching (*see also* Bishops) 135

Prejudice (*see also* Racial
   prejudice and injustice) 137
Pride 137
Procrastination (*see also*
   Starting) 138
Prophetic messages 139
Protection 140
Providence 140

Racial prejudice 142
Rainbows 144
Ransom 144
Redemption 145
Refugees (*see also* Cruelty) 145
Regeneration (*see also*
   Transformation) 146
Repentance 146
Rest 146
Retribution 146
Revival 146
Righteousness 149

Sacrifice (*see also* Jesus Christ:
   Jesus our sacrifice) 150
Saints 152
Salvation (*see also* Conversion;
   Jesus Christ; Ransom;
   Redemption) 153
Samaritans 154
Sanctification 155
Science (*see also* Discoveries) 156
Second coming: see Jesus Christ:
   Jesus' second coming 157
Self-promotion 157
Service (see also God: Serving
   God/Christ) 157
Signs and wonders:
   see Miracles 158
Sin 158
Social action (*see also* Poverty) 158
Sowing and reaping 161
Starting (*see also*
   Procrastination) 161

Stewardship: *see* Giving to God 161
Study 161
Success 161
Suffering (*see also* Torture;
   Tragedy) 163
Sunday 164

Talents 165
Tears 165
Television 166
Temper 166
Temptation 167
Theology 167
Time 168
Torture 168
Tragedy 168
Transformation (*see also*
   Regeneration) 169
Treasure 169
Trees 169
Trinity 169
Trusting God 169
Truth 171
Twentieth century 171

Unity 172

Visions 174
Vocation 175

Will of God: *see* God: The will of
   God 176
Wisdom 176
Witness, witnessing (*see also*
   Martyrdom; Persecution) 176
Women 177
Work (*see also* Dedication;
   Vocation) 178
Workaholism 178
World, end of the 179
Worry 179
Worship 180
Writing 180

Introduction

The Ultimate Speakers' Handbook is a resource book for speakers, preachers and teachers of the Christian faith. Stories are used to great effect in business management books and as case histories in counselling books. They have been used to communicate Christian truth ever since Jesus encapsulated much of his teaching in the form of parables, and even before then, in the pages of the Old Testament.

This is not a manual on 'How to tell stories'. All Christian preachers and teachers who need help in this area would benefit from reading a book like Jeanette Perkins Brown's *The Storyteller in Religious Education* (Chester Houses Publications, 1956). Perhaps the greatest hindrance to effective communication by preachers and teachers of the Christian faith today is the fact that so many of them do not realize how ineffectively they are communicating. They become so used to preaching and teaching that they fail to ask, 'How much of this is getting across to my audience/congregation?'

Communications experts tell us that our sight gives us 83 per cent of our total sensory input, our hearing gives us 11 per cent, our sense of smell gives us 4 per cent and our sense of taste gives us 2 per cent. Obviously, our sight and our hearing are our most important senses. The figures below show how much of their input we remember:

	After 3 hours	After 3 days
Hearing only	70%	10%
Sight only	72%	20%
Hearing and sight	85%	65%

This does not mean that every talk or sermon must have a video or visual aid, but it does suggest that the spoken word is remembered more easily if the hearer is able to visualize it and 'see' what the speaker is saying. It is not difficult to see how many sermons would be greatly improved with the addition of an appropriate story or two.

Quotations, sayings and proverbs add spice and interest to any talk or sermon. Winston Churchill believed that books of quotations had their uses: 'Every man like myself, who never went to college, can largely make up for that lack by reading the wise sayings of the great men of the past, who gladly left their wisdom and experience in proverbs for us who follow.' Professor Toynbee has said, 'One of the greatest treasures is a collection of wise sayings and proverbs for sharpening the mind.' Alexander Graham Bell, the inventor of telephones, gave this advice about proverbs:

'Fire your ambition and courage by studying the priceless advice in the proverbs and wise sayings. They're the shortest road to wisdom you'll ever find.'

Apt quotations can be used to great effect in any sermon or talk. Often, the quotation may say something which is obvious, but because it was said by somebody clever, famous or learned, it is listened to with more respect than the words of a local preacher!

The sources of the stories and quotations in this book range from contemporary entertainers and sporting heroes to theologians, preachers, philosophers and missionaries from many centuries. Included are a number of well-known conversion stories, some accounts of Christian martyrdoms and some stories from revivals in different centuries. Also included are many traditional illustrations such as those of John Bunyan, which still illuminate and explain themes and particular verses in the Bible.

Every preacher has one purpose: to help his hearers to understand and absorb Christian truth. His aim is not to tell gripping stories and throw out memorable quotations merely so that everyone will think he is clever, humorous and learned. The Puritan theologian James Denny gave this advice to preachers: 'No preacher can at one and the same time give the impression that he is clever and that Jesus is great and wonderful.'

Robert Backhouse
Norwich, 1997

ABORTION

A woman went to her doctor in Bonn, seeking an abortion. Of her previous children, the first was blind, the second had died, the third was deaf and dumb, and the fourth, like her mother, had TB. The doctor was not at all hopeful that the fifth child would be healthy. In today's climate of opinion many people would have advised the woman that she had very strong grounds for having an abortion. Had she done so the composer Beethoven would not have been born.

We are fighting abortion by adoption. We have sent word to the clinics, to the hospitals, to the police stations. 'Please do not destroy the child. We will take the child.'
Mother Teresa of Calcutta (Nobel Peace Prize lecture, 1970)

ABSTINENCE

Total abstinence is easier for me than perfect moderation.
Augustine

ACHIEVEMENT

The Great Wall of China is the largest thing that has ever been built. The original wall was built by the Emperor Shih Huang Ti to keep invaders out of China. The final wall stretched for over 2,400 kilometres.

ACTION

See also **Faith**
Action may not always bring happiness; but there is no happiness without action.
Benjamin Disraeli

He who desires but acts not breeds pestilence.
He who would do good to another must do it in minute particulars.
William Blake

Nobody makes a greater mistake than he who does nothing because he could only do a little.
Edmund Burke

He who passively accepts evil is as much involved in it as he who helps to perpetrate it.
Author unknown

We are not made righteous by doing righteous deeds; but when we have been made righteous we do righteous deeds.
Martin Luther

No man has a right to lead such a life of contemplation as to forget in his own ease the service due to his neighbour; nor has any man a right to be so immersed in active life as to neglect the contemplation of God.
Augustine

To give our Lord a perfect hospitality, Mary and Martha must combine.
Teresa of Avila

ADORATION
See also **God**
The most fundamental need, duty, honour and happiness of mankind is not petition, nor even contrition, nor again even thanksgiving – these three kinds of prayer which, indeed, must never disappear out of our spiritual lives – but adoration.
Friedrich von Hugel

ADULTERY
In 1631 Robert Barker and Martin Lucas, the King's printers in London, printed an edition of the Bible with numerous mistakes in it. In this edition the seventh commandment read: 'Thou shalt commit adultery.' Consequently this version of the Bible became known as 'the Wicked Bible'. King Charles I had all of its 1,000 copies recalled and fined the printers £3,000.

Jerry Adler in *Newsweek* described a change in the American view of adultery: 'The new understanding of adultery is that it is a sin of the heart more than the body.' According to Dr Frank Pitman, adultery consists of engaging in 'a secret intimacy with someone' – an intimacy which is then lied about. A man from New Jersey sued his wife for divorce, claiming that she was having an adulterous affair with a man whom she had never met but to whom she sent 'racy computer messages'.
Newsweek (5 October 1996)

ADVICE

Advice is like snow. The softer it falls, the easier it's absorbed, the deeper it sinks, and the longer it lasts.
Author unknown

AMBITION

See also **Contentment**

Russel Harty, a popular chat-show host in the 1980s, was quite frank about his ambition: 'I want to be very, very rich. I want to be so rich it really hurts. I want a deep, vast reservoir of money which would buy me freedom. Then I think I would go back to being a school teacher, as I used to be in Giggleswick.'

I would rather be Head of the Ragged Schools than have the command of armies.
Lord Shaftesbury

Oprah Winfrey, the highly successful American chat-show host, has given this advice: 'Think like a queen. A queen is not afraid to fail. Failure is another stepping-stone to greatness.' An audience of 90 million people watched her live interview with the pop star Michael Jackson. She gives $50,000 a year so that the people of Alexandria in South Africa can have a meal every day.

Damon Hill, the 1996 Formula 1 racing world champion, said, 'Winning is everything. The only ones who remember when you come second are your wife and your dog.'

> Cromwell, I charge thee, fling away ambition:
> By that sin fell the angels. How can man then,
> The image of his maker, hope to win by it?
>
> *William Shakespeare (Henry VIII)*

'You know, I'm a pretty stable person overall, but last week I learned the biggest lesson yet: Just say no!' So said supermodel Jenny McCarthy, who, over a seven-day period, turned down an MTV offer and said 'not now' to NBC and Fox TV. She was holding out for her own variety/comedy show, and she finally got what she wanted. *The Jenny McCarthy Show* went on the air in 1997.

ANGELS

One night hostile natives surrounded the mission headquarters of John Paton, a missionary in the New Hebrides Islands. They were bent on setting fire to the buildings and killing Paton. He and his wife prayed for deliverance through the night. In the morning they were amazed when the natives withdrew, for no apparent reason.

The chief of these natives subsequently became a Christian, and about a year after this frightening night Paton asked the chief why his men had not killed him. The chief replied, 'How could we, with all the men you had on your side?'

Paton replied, 'But there was nobody with us! There was just my wife and I.'

The chief then went on to describe the men who had guarded the mission headquarters. 'There were hundreds of very strong men, with drawn swords in their hands, wearing clothes that shone. They completely surrounded your compound so that we could not attack.'

Then Paton realized that God had answered their prayers that night with protecting angels.

ANGER

A man is as big as the things that make him angry.

Winston Churchill

Anybody can become angry – that is easy; but to be angry with the right person, and to the right degree, and at the right time, and for the right purpose, and in the right way – that is not within everybody's power and it is not easy.

Aristotle

Once I got past my anger toward my mother, I began to excel in volleyball and modelling.
Gabrielle Reece (supermodel)

ANGLICANISM
The merit of the Anglican Church is, that if you let it alone, it will let you alone.
Ralph Waldo Emerson

ANIMALS
I believe that mink are raised for being turned into fur coats and if we didn't wear fur coats those little animals would never have been born. So is it better not to have been born or to have lived for a year or two to have been turned into a fur coat? I don't know.
Barbi Benton (supermodel)

A freak wave hit 28-year-old Doris Svorinic while she was snorkelling in the sea at Durban, South Africa, in 1997. She was winded by this and sank under the waves. By the time she managed to surface she was so tired that she started to hyperventilate and could not swim. She was certain that she would drown. But just then some dolphins came to her rescue. They lifted her up from underneath and carried her safely to the shore.

Donald Mottram, a farmer in Dyfed, Wales, lay unconscious for 90 minutes in a field after he had been gored and trampled by an angry bull. But his herd of cows – marshalled by his favourite cow, a 14-year-old called Daisy – came to the rescue. They encircled him to keep the bull away, and he was eventually able to crawl the 200 yards to a gate, while the cows shielded him. 'They knew of the danger and decided to protect me,' he explained.

ANXIETY
See **Worry**

APOSTLES
I do not, as Peter and Paul, issue commandments to you. They were apostles; I am just a condemned man.
Ignatius of Antioch (AD 110)

ARGUMENTS

Helen Waddell tells the story of two old men who lived in the desert in order to give themselves to a life of holy living and prayer:

There were two old men living in one cell, and never had there risen even the paltriest contention between them. So the one said to the other, 'Let us have one quarrel, the way other men do.'

But the other said, 'I do not know how one makes a quarrel.'

The first said, 'Look, I set a tile between us and say, "That is mine," and do thou say, "It is not thine, it is mine," and thence arise contention and squabble.'

So they set the tile between them; and the first one said, 'That is mine,' and the second made reply: 'I hope that it is mine.'

To which the first made answer, 'If it is thine, take it.' After which they could find no way of quarrelling.

Never answer an angry word with an angry word. It's always the second remark that starts the trouble.

Author unknown

ARMINIANISM

When I come to a text which speaks of election, I delight myself in the doctrine of election. When the apostles exhort me to repentance and obedience, and indicate my freedom of choice and action, I give myself up to that side of the question.

Charles Simeon

ASSURANCE

In his famous book *The Pilgrim's Progress* John Bunyan tells the story of Mr Fearing, a pilgrim on his journey to the Celestial City. This was a man who 'had the root of the matter in him' but, as Mr Honest says of him, 'he was one of the most troublesome pilgrims that ever I met with in all my days.' So what was so wrong with Mr Fearing?

His name says it all, but his travelling companion, Mr Great-heart, fills in the details. Mr Fearing 'was always afraid that he should come short of whither he had a desire to go. Everything frightened him that he heard anybody speak of, that had but the least appearance of opposition in it.' It was not simply that he had external difficulties to face – all pilgrims meet with those – it was that he had 'a Slough of Despond in his mind, a slough that he carried everywhere with him or else he could never have been as he was.'

He was oppressed by a sense of his own unworthiness and hung back when he was invited to go forward, letting others go in front of him. But he was not daunted greatly by dangerous obstacles. When he came to the Hill Difficulty, he had no problem about climbing it, nor did he much fear the lions: 'his trouble was not about such things as those; his fear was about his acceptance at last.'

But at the very end of his journey he acquired a new boldness. The water of the river was lower than Mr Great-heart had ever seen it. So Mr Fearing 'went over at last, not much over wetshod'. When he was going up to the gate Mr Great-heart began to take his leave of him and to wish him a good reception above.

Thus the once doubting pilgrim arrived at his destination, triumphant in the end. His greatest difficulty had always been that 'he had some doubts about his interest in that celestial country'. But he did arrive at his destination, despite his struggles within himself, for 'the root of the matter was in him' and he would never turn back. Bunyan still speaks to tender consciences and doubting minds through his Mr Fearing.

ATHEISM

Isaac Newton, a strong Christian believer, was a professor of mathematics at Cambridge University for 32 years at the end of the seventeenth century. He became renowned for discovering the laws of planetary motion and gravitation. One day an atheist friend came into his room. In it was an orrery, a clockwork model which showed how the planets moved around the sun. Newton's friend admired the beautiful and complicated orrery and asked him who had made it. Newton replied, 'Nobody made it. It just happened.'

A nineteenth-century atheist was determined that his daughter should not acquire any mistaken religious ideas as she grew up. He knew that when she went into the homes of some of her school-friends she would see Bible texts hanging on the walls, for such was the fashion of the age. To counter this, while the girl was still very young and not yet able to read, he hung in their living room a text that read simply: 'God is nowhere.'

Some months later the little girl surprised her father by telling him that she could read 'the writing on the wall'. Proudly, slowly and syllable by syllable, she read it out: 'God is now here.'

Atheism turns out to be too simple. If the whole universe has no meaning, we should have never found out that it has no meaning.
C. S. Lewis (Mere Christianity)

The complete atheist stands on the penultimate step to most perfect faith (he may or may not take a further step), but the indifferent person has no faith whatever except a bad fear, and that but rarely, and only if he is sensitive.
Fyodor Dostoevsky

Belief is a wise wager. Granted that faith cannot be proved, what harm will come to you if you gamble on its truth and it proves false? If you gain, you gain all; if you lose, you lose nothing. Wager, then, without hesitation, that God exists.
Blaise Pascal

BACKSLIDING

Those who fall away have never been thoroughly imbued with the knowledge of Christ but only had a slight and passing taste of it.
John Calvin

BAPTISM

Baptism can be looked at from two points of view. From our point of view, we see it as the time when we publicly witness to our faith in the Lord Jesus Christ. From God's point of view, our baptism is his acceptance of us. It is God saying to us, 'You are now a member of my family, thanks to my Son, Jesus Christ.'

Martin Luther is usually remembered as the man of faith who set Europe alight during the Reformation through his strong emphasis on justification by faith. However, he was not immune to times of doubt and depression. During those times he did not say: 'I have been justified by faith.' Rather, he said: 'I have been baptized.' He recalled God's gracious act of adopting him. He remembered his baptism as the mark and sign of God accepting him. In his moments of doubt this spiritual giant remembered God's acceptance of him – dramatized in his baptism – rather than his acceptance of Christ.

BEAUTY

The being of all things is derived from the divine beauty.
Thomas Aquinas

Beauty is God's handwriting. Welcome it in every fair face, every fair day, every fair flower.
Charles Kingsley

The 1997 Miss Universe, Alicia Machado, comes from Venezuela. During the last 17 years that country has produced four Miss Universes and five Miss Worlds. Venezuela runs a Miss Venezuela Academy which takes young women from the streets of Caracas and, through fitness training, surgery, dentistry and lessons in physical and personal development, prepares them to enter major beauty contests.

Jennifer Aniston was paid $100,000 for each of her appearances in the American TV sitcom *Friends* during 1997. She is rated by many as the Farrah Fawcett-Majors of the nineties. She says she doesn't think of herself as a sex symbol, and when she sees her picture on a magazine cover she doesn't see herself but someone who has been 'painted, fluffed, puffed and done-up'.

Millions of other women have copied Jennifer's hair-style, which has been described as 'America's First Hairdo, a semi-sculpted, semi-tousled shoulder-length affair'. She says she doesn't know what all the fuss is about, as her friend Chris 'took a razor blade and just chopped'.

BECOMING A CHRISTIAN
See **Conversion**

BEHAVIOUR
The Russian neuropsychologist, Professor Pavlov, devoted his whole life to the study of human behaviour. His most famous experiment involved a number of dogs which were used to demonstrate the conditioned reflex. Pavlov had noticed how dogs produce saliva as soon as they are shown food. He rang a bell just before he fed the dogs in this experiment. It wasn't long before he could ring the bell and the dogs started to salivate, whether or not they received food.

He went on to repeat this experiment in two other ways. He shone a light and touched the dogs' bodies in the same spot just before they were fed. Once again the dogs produced saliva whenever the light shone or whenever they were touched, irrespective of whether they were fed. From these observations Pavlov developed his theory of the conditioned reflex.

Many people (including Christians, in some instances) are also governed by conditioned reflexes. Faced with a moral problem, we just react to it rather than thinking it through rationally.

BELIEF
I can see how it might be possible for a man to look down upon the earth and be an atheist, but I cannot conceive how he could look up into the heavens and say there is no God.
Abraham Lincoln

BEREAVEMENT
See also **Death**; **Dying**

My little daughter Elizabeth is dead. She has left me wonderfully sick at heart and almost womanish. I am so moved by pity for her. I could never have believed a father's heart could be so tender for his child. Pray to God for me.
Martin Luther

BIBLE
See also **Job, book of**

Back to the Bible, or back to the jungle.
Luis Palau

Scripture is above our natural reason, understanding, and comprehension.
Justin Martyr

Defend the Bible? I would as soon defend a lion! Unchain it and it will defend itself.
C. H. Spurgeon

The devil can cite scripture for his purpose.
William Shakespeare (Antonio in The Merchant of Venice*)*

No public man in these islands ever believes that the Bible means what it says; he is always convinced that it says what he means.
George Bernard Shaw

Christ in the Bible

Every word in the Bible rings with Christ.
Martin Luther

We come to a cradle in order to see a baby, so we come to the Bible to see Christ.
Martin Luther

Knowledge of scripture is knowledge of Christ and ignorance of them is ignorance of him.

Jerome

Some people say, 'Unless I find it in the scriptures I will not believe it in the gospel.' And when I tell them that it *is* in the scriptures, they say, 'That remains to be proved.' But as far as I am concerned, Jesus Christ *is* the scriptures: you cannot alter his cross, death and resurrection, and faith through him.

Ignatius of Antioch

The influence of the Bible

In 1787 one of His Majesty's transport ships sailed from Spithead. The ship was the *Bounty*, and Captain Bligh was its captain. On board were 25 very rough-and-ready sailors who came to hate Captain Bligh because he was such a strict disciplinarian.

They sailed to the South Seas to collect a tropical fruit known as breadfruit, which had white flesh and a bread-like texture. When they landed at Tahiti they thought they were in paradise. They were surrounded by blue seas, golden sands and glamorous girls. Before long every sailor had his own girlfriend and, to the sailors' delight, they stayed there for several months. Captain Bligh made himself even more unpopular when he suddenly announced one day that they were going to set sail the next day! Fletcher Christian, one of the officers, complained about this and had secret meetings with the sailors. They talked about a mutiny, about killing Captain Bligh and getting rid of the *Bounty*.

However, the ship did set sail. But a few days later Fletcher Christian masterminded a mutiny and tied up Bligh. Christian and the mutineers sailed back to Tahiti to collect their girlfriends, who willingly sailed off to sea with them. When they came across Pitcairn Island (an uninhabited extinct volcano island with lush vegetation) they went ashore and took everything they could from the *Bounty*, and then they set fire to her.

On Pitcairn Island they looked forward to paradise on earth, but they soon found themselves living in a kind of hell. One of the mutineers used the old copper kettle from the *Bounty* to rig up a distillery, and he used tree roots to make spirits. Soon the sailors and women became drunk and remained that way for days, weeks and even months on end. Some of the men became like animals, fighting among themselves. One committed suicide by flinging himself over the edge of a volcanic cliff.

After several years only two men were left, Edward Young and Alexander Smith. Young was an older man, seriously ill with asthma. The women, with the 18 children who had been born to them, seized the guns one night and barricaded themselves in. The two sailors were left to live their lives on their own, and none of the women or children would go near them.

Young realized that he was dying. One day he went along to the ship's chest and rummaged around in it. At the bottom, among a pile of old papers, he found an old, leather-bound, worm-eaten, mildewed book. It was the *Bounty*'s Bible.

He had not read anything for years. He started to read at the beginning of Genesis. He also taught his friend Lex to read. These two wrecks of humanity read the Bible together for many hours each day. They prayed, as best they could. They sought light and guidance for all they were worth from the pages of the Old Testament.

The little children were the first to come back as they noticed the change in the men. Then the women came back, and they sat around in a circle while Edward, and sometimes Lex, read to them. When they came to the Psalms they realized that they were hymns, and so in their own very strange way they started to sing the Psalms together.

Edward died peacefully in his sleep one night. Lex kept on reading the Bible. When he came to the New Testament he said, 'I had been working like a mole for years, and suddenly it was as if the doors were flung wide open, and I saw the light, and I met God in Jesus Christ. And the burden of my sin rolled away, and I found new life in Christ.'

After they had been on Pitcairn Island for 18 years, a boat from Boston came across the island, and the captain landed. He found a quiet, godly community, characterized by a grace and a peace that he had never before seen. Their leader greeted the captain: 'I am Alexander Smith. I am the only survivor from the *Bounty*. If you want to arrest me, you can.'

The captain replied, 'I don't know anything about the *Bounty*, but what I do know is that these people here clearly need you.' Before he left the island Lex told him every detail about the last 18 years of his life.

When the captain returned to the United States he reported that in all his travels he had never met another group of people who were so good and so loving. He knew that there was only one book which could produce a miracle like that.

Dr J. N. Darby preached the gospel among the poor farming families of Ireland for many years. One day, a well-known unbeliever challenged Darby's faithful preaching: 'You claim that all scripture is profitable. But what possible earthly value is a verse like 2 Timothy 4:13, "When you come, bring the cloak that I left with Carpus at Troas, and my scrolls, especially the parchments"?'

Darby replied: 'Did you know that when I left my previous work to come and live here it was this particular verse that kept me from selling all my theological books? Make no mistake about it, all scripture is inspired by God and it is all profitable.'

The sacred books are pervaded by the Spirit. There is nothing either in the prophets, on in the law, or in the gospels, or in the epistles, which does not spring from the fullness of the divine majesty.
Origen

Mary Queen of Scots asked, 'Ye interpret the scriptures in one manner, and they in another; whom shall I believe, and who shall judge?'

The preacher John Knox replied, 'Believe God, that plainly speaketh in his word: and further than the word teacheth you, ye shall neither believe the one nor the other. The word of God is plain in itself; and if there appear any obscurity in one place, the Holy Ghost, which is never contrarious to himself, explains the same more clearly in other places.'

Opposition to the Bible

Man's hatred of the Bible has been of a most persistent, determined, relentless and bitter character. Over the centuries repeated attempts have been made to undermine faith in the Bible, and to consign the Bible itself to oblivion. These attempts have utterly failed.

Celsus tried it with the brilliance of his genius, and he failed. Porphyry tried it with the depth of subtlety of his philosophy, and he failed. Lucian tried it with the keenness of his satire, and he failed.

Then other weapons were used. Diocletian, the mightiest ruler of the mightiest empire in the world, brought to bear against the Bible all the power of Rome. He issued edicts that every Bible should be burned, but that failed. Then he issued an edict that all who possessed a Bible should be put to death. But even that failed.

So for centuries the assault upon the Bible was continued. Every type of destruction that human philosophy, human science, human reason, human art, human cunning, human force, and human brutality could bring to bear against a book has been brought to bear against this Book, and yet the Bible stands absolutely unshaken today. At times almost all

the wise and great of the earth have been pitted against the Bible, and only an obscure few for it. Yet it has stood.
R. A. Torrey

Bible reading

By reading the scriptures I am so renewed that all nature seems renewed around me and with me. The sky seems to be a pure, a cooler blue, the trees a deeper green ... The whole world is charged with the glory of God and I feel fire and music ... under my feet.
Thomas Merton

York Minster has a famous stained-glass window called 'The Five Sisters' which is the largest of its kind in Europe. From the outside it is totally disappointing, as all you can see is a dull expanse of dark glass. But from the inside, with the light streaming through it, one sees its exquisite beauty.

Viewed from the outside by non-believers, the Bible's message is easy to miss. But if it is read from the inside by a prayerful Christian, its pages are lit up by God himself.

The vigour of our spiritual life will be in exact proportion to the place held by the Bible in our life and thoughts.
George Müller

The holy scriptures are that divine instrument by which we are taught what to believe, concerning God, ourselves, and all things, and how to please God unto eternal life.
John Robinson

I began to read the holy scriptures upon my knees, laying aside all other books, and praying over, if possible, every line and word. This proved meat indeed and drink indeed to my soul. I daily received fresh life, light and power from above.
George Whitefield (Journal)

Most people are bothered by the passages of scripture which they cannot understand; but as for me, I have always noticed that the passages in scripture which trouble me most are those which I do understand.
Mark Twain

Read the Bible, first and foremost, always, every day, unremittingly and often with a concordance, until the history and prophecy and the wisdom literature of the Old Testament get into our very bones; and until the Gospels and Epistles of the New Testament become the foundation blocks of our thinking and way of life.
John S. Higgins (American bishop)

The Bible applied to the heart by the Holy Spirit, is the chief means by which men are built up and established in the faith, after their conversion.
J. C. Ryle

The soul can do nothing without the word of God, and the soul can manage without anything except the word of God.
Martin Luther

BIRTHDAYS

Alexander the Great, Julius Caesar, Plato and Philip Melancthon, the Reformer, all died on their birthdays. John Huss, the martyr, was burned at the stake on his birthday.

Charles Kingsley, the writer, was on holiday at the seaside on his birthday when he gave his life to Christ. So his second birth was on the same date as his first birth.

The world's most tragic birthday party took place in King Herod's palace, when he promised his niece Herodias anything she wanted. She asked for John the Baptist's head on a plate.

A boy had three presents on his birthday: a box of chocolates, a silver watch and a beautiful Bible. A few weeks later he was asked what had happened to his presents. He replied, 'The box of chocolates has gone, the watch is still going, but the Bible is the Word of the Lord, and it endures for ever.'

BISHOPS

A bishop was complaining to the king about the unusual activities of George Whitefield, advising him what steps should be taken to stop his preaching. His majesty replied, 'My Lord, I can see no other way but for us to make a bishop of him. This will stand a good chance of stopping his wild career.'

BLINDNESS

See also **Endurance; Suffering**

Helen Keller became blind and deaf at the age of 19 months after catching scarlet fever. In later life she said: 'It gives me a deep comforting sense that "Things seen are temporal and things unseen are eternal." '

Spiritual blindness

The very limit of human blindness is to glory in being blind.

Augustine

A man once stood up on a soap-box at Hyde Park Corner, pouring scorn on Christianity:

'People tell me that God exists; but I can't see him. People tell me that there is a life after death; but I can't see it. People tell me that there is a judgement to come; but I can't see it. People tell me that there is a heaven and a hell; but I can't see them.'

He won some cheap applause, and climbed down from his 'pulpit'. Then another man struggled on to the soap-box.

'People tell me that there is green grass all around, but I can't see it. People tell me that there is blue sky above, but I can't see it. People tell me that there are trees nearby, but I can't see them. You see, I'm blind.'

BROTHERHOOD

Before the Berlin Wall was demolished in 1989, someone had written this slogan on it: 'Live alone and free, like a tree, but in the brotherhood of the forest.'

BULIMIA

According to the Institute of Psychiatry in London and Boston University, between 1988 and 1993 the number of people suffering from the eating disorder bulimia went up threefold, from 15 to 50 out of every 100,000. Dr Janet Treasure of the Institute of Psychiatry said the increase had to do with 'the culture of thinness and weight-watching... It's also a way people now find of expressing distress... People feel they need to solve all their problems themselves and they develop bulimia as a way of dealing with them.'

Reported in The Week

BUSYBODIES
See also **Gossip**

'If everybody minded their own business,' the Duchess said in a hoarse growl, 'the world would go round a deal faster than it does.'

Lewis Carroll (Alice in Wonderland)

CALLING

See also **Mission**

The awareness of a need and the capacity to meet that need: this constitutes a call.
John R. Mott

My boyfriend thinks I lost my true calling to be a librarian.
Paulina Porizkova (supermodel)

CHALLENGE

I have nothing to offer but blood, toil, tears, and sweat.
Winston Churchill (May 1940)

Soldiers, all our efforts against superior forces have been unavailing. I have nothing to offer you but hunger and thirst, hardship and death; but I call on all who love their country to join with me.
Garibaldi (after the siege of Rome in 1849)

CHANCE

Random chance seems to have operated in our favour.
Mr Spock in Star Trek

CHARACTER

In war, three quarters turn on personal character and relations; the balance of manpower and materials counts only for the remaining quarter.
Napoleon

Character is better than ancestry, and personal conduct is more important than the highest parentage.
Thomas Barnardo

Fame is a vapour, popularity is an accident, and money takes wings. The only thing that endures is character.
O. J. Simpson

CHILDREN
See also **Discipline; Family life**

The sixteenth-century Spanish Jesuit missionary Francis Xavier Loyola said: 'Give me the children until they are seven and anyone may have them afterwards.' He also said: 'Give us the child, and we will give you the man.'

> If a child lives with criticism,
>   he learns to condemn.
> If a child lives with hostility,
>   he learns to fight.
> If a child lives with fear,
>   he learns to be apprehensive.
> If a child lives with pity,
>   he learns to feel sorry for himself.
> If a child lives with jealousy,
>   he learns to feel guilty.
> If a child lives with encouragement,
>   he learns to be self-confident.
> If a child lives with tolerance,
>   he learns to be patient.
> If a child lives with praise,
>   he learns to be appreciative.
> If a child lives with acceptance,
>   he learns to love.
> If a child lives with approval,
>   he learns to like himself.
> If a child lives with recognition,
>   he learns to have a goal.
> If a child lives with fairness,
>   he learns what justice is.
> If a child lives with honesty,
>   he learns what truth is.
> If a child lives with sincerity,
>   he learns to have faith in himself and those around him.
> If a child lives with love,
>   he learns that the world is a wonderful place to live in.

Author unknown

Love God.
Thrust down pride.
Forgive gladly.
Be sober of meat and drink.
Use honest company.
Reverence thine elders.
Trust in God's mercy.
Be always occupied.
Lose no time.
Falling down, despair not.
Ever take a fresh, new purpose.
Persevere constantly.
Wash clean.
Be no sluggard.
Awake quickly.
Enrich thee with virtue.
Learn diligently.
Teach what thou hast learned lovingly.
John Colet (Catechism for Children)

Give us the child for eight years and it will be a Bolshevik for ever.
Lenin (to the Commissars of Education in Moscow, 1923)

Over-indulgent love towards children can spoil them. This document issued by the Police Department of Houston, Texas clearly illustrates this:

Twelve Rules for Spoiling a Child
1) Begin at infancy to give the child everything he wants. In this way he will grow up to believe that the world owes him a living.
2) When he picks up bad words laugh at him. This will make him think he's cute.
3) Never give him any spiritual training. Wait until he is 21 and then let him decide for himself.
4) Avoid the use of the word 'wrong'. The child may develop a guilt complex. This will condition him to believe later, when arrested for stealing a car, that society is against him and that he's being persecuted.
5) Pick up everything he leaves lying around – books, shoes, clothes. Do everything for him so that he will be experienced in throwing all responsibility on other people.

6) Let him read any printed material he can get his hands on. Be careful that his silverwear and drinking glasses are sterilized, but let his mind feed on garbage.

7) Quarrel frequently in the presence of your children. In this way they will not be too shocked when the home is broken up later.

8) Give a child all the spending money he wants. Never let him earn his own. Why should he have things as tough as you had them?

9) Satisfy every craving for food, drink and comfort. See that every sensual desire is satisfied. Denial may lead to harmful frustration.

10) Take his part against neighbours, teachers, policemen. They are all prejudicial against your child.

11) When he gets into real trouble apologize for him yourself by saying, 'I never could do anything with him.'

12) Prepare for a life of grief. You will be likely to have it.

At that time Jesus said, 'I praise you, Father, Lord of heaven and earth, because you have hidden these things from the wise and learned, and revealed them to little children'.
(Matthew 11:25)

A child of five would understand this. Send someone to fetch a child of five.
Groucho Marx (in Duck Soup*)*

CHRIST
See **Jesus Christ**

CHRISTIANITY
Christianity is different from all other religions. They are the story of man's search for God. The Gospel is the story of God's search for man.
Dewi Morgan (former rector of St Bride's, Fleet Street, London)

CHRISTLIKENESS
It's not great talents that God blesses, but great likeness to Jesus.
Robert Murray M'Cheyne

CHURCH

In the Chinese city of Chungking, Bibles, prayer books and hymn books were all seized and burned in public during the Cultural Revolution of the 1960s. The local Christians were forced to watch these bonfires. While a Red Guard's attention was distracted, one of the Christians made the most of the opportunity and snatched out of the flames whatever his hand could grasp. He managed to save one page of the Bible. For years, the underground church in Chungking read and re-read this single page of God's Word.

When the Romanian Baptist church leader Richard Wurmbrand first heard this story he longed to know what page from the Bible they had. After two years he discovered that they had read each Sunday the words, 'On this rock will I build my church.' The much-tortured and long-imprisoned Wurmbrand wrote, 'Neither Mao Tse Tung, nor the burying alive of Christians, nor the gouging out of eyes, nor the cutting out of tongues, nor the desecration of church buildings, nor the gates of hell shall prevail against Jesus' church.'

The church is the daughter of the Word, not the Word's mother.
Martin Luther

Before Christ comes it is useless to expect to see the perfect church.
J. C. Ryle

The day we find the perfect church, it becomes imperfect the moment we join it.
C. H. Spurgeon

There are many sheep without, many wolves within.
Augustine

He cannot have God for his Father who has not the church for his mother.
St Cyprian

For those to whom God is a Father, the Church must also be a mother.
John Calvin

Of course we believe in the invisible Church, evident to God's eye alone, but we are told to accept the visible Church and remain in communion with it.
John Calvin

COMFORT

A trifle consoles us because a trifle upsets us.
Blaise Pascal

God does not comfort us to make us comfortable, but to make us comforters.
J. H. Jowett

CONTENTMENT

In an interview in the *Daily Mail* newspaper Jimmy Saville, the British TV and radio entertainer, said: 'A kid's life now is full of acquisition. Mine was a more exciting existence because you woke up in the morning expecting nothing at all.'

The royal adviser Cineas was trying to stop the Greek king Pyrrhus from attacking the Romans. 'Sir,' said Cineas, 'when you have conquered them, what will you do next?'

Pyrrhus replied, 'I will conquer Sicily, as it is close and an easy target.'

'What will you do when you have conquered Sicily?' asked Cineas.

'Why, then, I will go on to Africa and take Carthage,' replied Pyrrhus enthusiastically.

'After you have conquered all this, what will you do then?' persisted Cineas.

'We will then go back to Greece and take back everything we have lost there,' answered Pyrrhus.

'When you have conquered everyone, what benefits do you expect to derive from all your victories?' asked Cineas.

'Then,' said Pyrrhus, 'we will be able to settle down and enjoy ourselves.'

'Sir,' said Cineas, 'may we not do this now? Do you not already possess a kingdom of your own? He who cannot enjoy himself with a kingdom will not be satisfied with the whole world.'

The field-mouse invited a friend who lived in a town house to have a meal with him in the country. The friend accepted at once. But when he found that the meal consisted only of barley and other corn, he said to his host: 'Let me tell you, my friend, you live like an ant. But I have so many good things to eat, and if you come to my home I will share them all with you.'

So the country mouse set off with the town mouse to his home. The town mouse showed his friend his beans and peas, bread, dates, cheese, honey, and fruit. The country mouse was amazed to see all this lovely food and congratulated the town mouse and cursed his own lot. Just as they were about to start their meal the door opened, and the timid creatures were so frightened by what they heard that they ran for their holes in the floor. When they returned and were just about to tuck into some dried figs, they saw someone else coming into the room to collect something, and once more had to dive for cover. The field-mouse decided that he would go home, even though he was still hungry.

'Good-bye, my friend,' he said, with a groan. 'You may eat until you are full and enjoy yourself. But your good food costs you dear in terms of danger and fear. I prefer to gnaw my poor meals of barley and corn without any fear or having to constantly keep on the watch for an intruder.'

Moral: A simple life with peace and quiet is better than eating the finest foods and being in the grip of fear.

One of Aesop's fables

CONVERSION

See also **Repentance**

One day, at the end of one of George Whitefield's meetings, a lady asked him: 'Mr Whitefield, why do you preach so much on "Ye must be born again"?' Whitefield replied, 'Because, Madam, ye must be born again.'

Just because you were born in a garage, it doesn't mean to say that you are a car.

Author unknown

The entrance fee into the kingdom of heaven is nothing: the annual subscription is everything.

Henry Drummond

He ran thus till he came to a place somewhat ascending; and upon that place stood a cross, and a little below in the bottom, a sepulchre. So I saw in my dream, that just as Christian came up to the cross, his burden loosed from off his shoulders, and fell from off his back; and began to tumble; and so continued to do, till it came to the mouth of the sepulchre, where it fell in, and I saw it no more.

Then was Christian glad and lightsome [i.e. light-hearted], and said with a merry heart, 'He hath given me rest, by his sorrow; and life, by his death.' Then he stood awhile to look and wonder; for it was very surprising to him, that the sight of the cross should thus ease him of his burden. He looked therefore, and looked again, even till the springs that were in his head sent the waters down his cheeks. Now as he stood looking and weeping, behold three shining ones came to him, and saluted him, with 'Peace be to thee.' The first said to him, 'Thy sins be forgiven.' The second stript him of his rags, and clothed him with a change of raiment. The third put a mark on his forehead, gave him a roll with a seal on it which he bid him look on as he ran, and that he should give it in at the Celestial Gate. So the three went their way. Then Christian gave three leaps for joy, and went on singing.

> Thus far did I come laden with my sin,
> Nor could ought ease the grief that I was in,
> Till I came hither: What a place this is!
> Must here be the beginning of my bliss?
> Must here the burden all from off my back?
> Must here the strings that bound it to me, crack?
> Blest cross! Blest sepulchre! Blest rather be
> The Man that there was put to shame for me.

John Bunyan (Pilgrim's Progress)

John Berridge, an eighteenth-century clergyman, wrote his own epitaph, which later appeared on his gravestone. It illustrates how he found Jesus Christ to be his own Saviour from sin, and how he wanted everyone else to make that same discovery:

> Here Lie
> The earthly remains of
> JOHN BERRIDGE,
> Late vicar of Everton,
> And an itinerant servant of Jesus Christ,
> Who loved His Master and His work,
> And after running on His errands many years
> Was called to wait on Him above.

READER,
No Salvation without new birth!
I was born in sin, February 1716.
Remained ignorant of my fallen state till 1730.
Lively proudly on faith and works for salvation till 1754.
Was admitted to Everton Vicarage, 1755.
Fled to Jesus alone for refuge, 1756.
Fell asleep in Christ, January 22, 1793.

David Watson often used to tell the following true story:

The Chaplain-General of the British Forces, Bishop Taylor Smith, was preaching in a great cathedral. In order to emphasize the necessity of new birth in Christ, he said: 'My dear people, do not substitute anything for the new birth. You may be a member of the Church, but Church membership is not new birth, for "Unless a person is born again he cannot see the kingdom of God." '

He then pointed towards the archdeacon who sat on his left in his stall and said: 'You might even be an Archdeacon like my friend in his stall and not be born again, for "Unless a person is born again he cannot see the kingdom of God." You might even be a bishop like myself, and not be born again, for "Unless a person is born again, he cannot see the kingdom of God." '

A few days later the bishop was surprised to receive this letter from the archdeacon:

> *My dear bishop: You have found me out. I have been a clergyman for over 30 years, but I have never known anything of the joy that Christians speak of. I never could understand it. Mine has been a hard legal service. I did not know what the matter was with me, but when you pointed directly to me, and said, 'You might even be an archdeacon and not be born again', I realized in a moment what the trouble was. I had never known anything of the new birth.*

The next day the bishop and the archdeacon met and spent some time reading the Bible together, after which they knelt down and the archdeacon acknowledged that he was a sinner and told Christ that he would trust him as his Saviour.

While Charles Spurgeon was the pastor at the Metropolitan Tabernacle in London he preached to over 5,000 people every Sunday, and over 14,000 new members joined this fellowship. Many thousands of others entered Christ's kingdom as a result of Spurgeon's faithful preaching. The following account of a converted thief is recorded in Spurgeon's *Autobiography*:

Some years ago, a father, living in a country town, apprenticed his son to a London Silversmith. For a time, all seemed to be going well; but, one day, he received a letter to say that the lad had robbed his master. The boy left in disgrace. The father collected his son and as they were walking through the crowded streets of the City of London, the lad suddenly ran off and disappeared. The police searched for him in vain, and the poor man had to return alone to tell the sad news to his broken-hearted wife.

Years passed, and nothing was heard of the prodigal son. One Sunday evening the parents stayed at home and prayed for their lost son. One of their servants came in from the church service, saying, 'Oh, sir! I have not heard a word of the sermon; I could do nothing but pray for Master Harry.'

That night, some men were passing the Metropolitan Tabernacle, on their way to break into a shop belonging to a London blacksmith, when one of them said, 'Harry, just run up the steps, and see the time.' He did so, opened the door, and stood in the aisle. Mr Spurgeon was preaching about the dying thief; and, seeming to point directly at Harry, said, 'If there is a thief here tonight, Jesus Christ can save him.'

The arrow hit the mark. Harry went back to his tumbled down home to pray. A week later he went and knocked on the door of his father's home. The father opened it, stood face to face with his lost son; and then followed the old story of the prodigal's return – tears, confession, forgiveness, welcome, restoration, joy.

Kriss Akabusi (British athlete)

Kriss Akabusi was happily married, and his success on the track was bringing him growing fame and financial security. But despite all this he was feeling dissatisfied. In 1985 his wife Monica gave birth to twin girls, but they both died at birth. Kriss started wondering what had happened to the girls, and where they now were. Also, he felt that his own life lacked meaning.

In 1986 he went to Edinburgh to take part in the Commonwealth Games. In his hotel room he found a New Testament written in everyday English, and he started to read it. He had heard about Jesus, but it had all seemed like a child's story. 'But when I opened up that Bible,' he says, 'I was confronted with Jesus... I had never realized that Jesus had walked on earth and that he had said so many amazing things.'

Kriss went home from Edinburgh determined to find out whether or not Jesus was an invented story. He read many books and asked many questions. The following April he went to America. 'On April 14th,' he says, 'I went to bed feeling very frustrated and said, "God, if you're really out there – Jesus, if you're really who you say you are – will you just let me know?" '

That night he had a dream. In it he saw Jesus saying, 'Come to me, those who are weary and heavy laden, and I will give you rest. For my yoke is easy and my burden is light.'

In his dream he called out, 'Jesus!' Then he woke up, feeling peaceful and happy. He wrote down his dream and fell asleep again. The next day all his doubts had gone. 'I knew God loved me – and that he loved everybody else as well.'

Augustine (fourth-century theologian)

In his famous autobiography *Confessions* Augustine describes how God's light penetrated the darkness of his soul at a time when he was greatly troubled in spirit and deeply challenged by the witness of Christians:

I threw myself down under a fig tree and collapsed in tears. 'How long, O Lord, how long will you be angry? For ever? Do not hold against us our former sins' [Psalms 79:5–8; 85:5] – for I felt I was bound by them. 'Tomorrow and tomorrow? Why not now? Why isn't there an end to my dirtiness here and now?'

I was talking like this and crying with most heartfelt bitterness when I heard a voice (perhaps a child's voice, I'm not sure) coming from a nearby house. It was chanting and repeating the words, 'Pick it up and read it!' Immediately my face changed and I began seriously to wonder whether children used these words in their games, but I couldn't remember ever hearing anything like them. So, subduing my tears, I got up, thinking it must be nothing other than a command from God to open the book and read the first chapter I found...

Then I ran back to where Alypius was sitting; for, when I left him, I had left the Apostle's book lying there. I picked it up, opened it, and silently read the passage [Romans 13:13–14] I first set eyes on: 'Let us behave decently, as in the daytime, not in orgies and drunkenness, not in sexual immorality and debauchery, not in dissension and jealousy. Rather, clothe yourselves with the Lord Jesus Christ, and do not think about how to gratify the desires of the sinful nature.'

I didn't want to read any further, and it wasn't necessary. As I reached the end of the sentence, the light of peace seemed to shine on my heart, and every shadow of doubt disappeared.

William Carey (eighteenth-century Baptist missionary)

William Carey was apprenticed to a shoemaker, along with another young man named Thomas Warr. They would often argue over their different views about Christian doctrine. Carey was good with words, and could easily out-argue the less bookish Warr, but he found he got no lasting enjoyment from his victories. Warr's faith was real, and Carey knew it was a different thing from his own.

In 1779 a National Day of Prayer was called, as England was at war with Spain and France. Carey and Warr together went to join the prayer meeting in the small meeting-room of the local Dissenting congregation. One of the members read Hebrews 13:13: 'Let us go forth, therefore, unto him without the camp, bearing his reproach.' The words were familiar to Carey, but now they found a deep resonance in his heart. The world was still rejecting Christ, but Carey knew that he had to commit himself, not just intellectually but with his heart. This came as the climax of several weeks of soul-searching, and he realized that at last Christ had found him and given him peace.

William Dobbie (British soldier in India)

Samuel Hebich was a missionary whose work God had greatly blessed. Realizing the great spiritual need of the British soldiers in India during the last century (he called them the 'white heathen'), Hebich spent much of his time visiting the garrisons, and many officers and soldiers were led to the Lord through his ministry.

One hot, sultry day an officer named William Dobbie was lying in his room during the hottest hours, when he suddenly heard footsteps approaching. In walked Mr Hebich, unannounced. He was a strange-looking man, with a long, loose-hanging coat, a large hat and a huge umbrella.

After a short silence Hebich said, 'Get down the Book.' Dobbie knew immediately which Book Hebich meant, and he fetched his Bible, which he never read himself.

'Open the Book at the first chapter of Genesis and read the first two verses,' said Hebich.

Dobbie obeyed and read like an attentive pupil: 'In the beginning God created the heaven and the earth. And the earth was without form, and void; and darkness was upon the face of the deep. And the Spirit of God moved upon the face of the waters.'

'That will do! Now close the Book and we will pray,' said Hebich. So they knelt down and Hebich prayed, but Dobbie was in too much of a turmoil to listen to the prayer. After this, his strange visitor bowed and said farewell, shaking hands very solemnly before leaving.

The following day there was the sound of footsteps again, and Hebich appeared. The performance of the previous day was repeated. Hebich was totally at ease, but his pupil was greatly embarrassed. Again Dobbie was asked to read the first two verses of Genesis. As before, the two men knelt down and prayed together, but this time Dobbie listened to the prayer. It was a kind of prayer he had never heard of before. Hebich prayed as if he was talking to an intimate friend, as he told his God and Father all about the young officer, asking God to reveal to him his need, so that he might find salvation from the open arms of the Redeemer. As before Hebich left in the same solemn way.

The Bible was left open on the table. Dobbie read those wonderful verses again, and now they began to have a powerful effect on him. Like a pupil who had been sent back to his lesson, he sat down and read those verses yet again. Now they burned into his soul. He was the 'void' and he was 'without form' – sin had made him like that. And the 'darkness' of indifference and unbelief had acted like a fog, so that he had been unable to see his utter ruin, and God's love. 'And the Spirit of God moved upon the face of the waters.' Dobbie wondered if, by his words and his prayers, this strange man Hebich had brought him into contact with the living God?

The next day he heard those same footsteps. This time Dobbie had his Bible open, as he waited for his teacher. He stood up to greet Hebich, took his hand and said, 'Oh, Mr Hebich, it is all clear to me now. What must I do?'

Looking at him with true love, Hebich said: 'My son, we hear that God said, "Let there be light", "Believe in the Lord Jesus Christ and thou shalt be saved." ' Then they knelt for prayer, and for the first time in his life the young officer prayed, without a book, from the heart. He had found life and peace, and he thanked God for his great salvation – the gift of eternal life through Christ.

The man converted in this story was the grandfather of Lieutenant-General Sir William Dobbie, the famous commander who valiantly defended Malta during World War II, and who himself was well known for being an outstanding Christian.

James Fox (British actor)

'Let yourself go' was the advice which the British actor James Fox had received from some of his friends – but he wasn't sure that was right. In fact, he felt that this way led to a horrible black abyss which would destroy him.

Searching for a positive alternative, he recalled from his public school chapel days the verse, 'Come unto me, all ye who labour and are heavy-laden, and I will give you rest' (Matthew 11:28). He tried living a decent life, and he went to Communion on Sundays. But he found this boring, and he had nobody to help him.

While performing in a play in Blackpool, he met a man at his hotel's breakfast table. Fox asked him what he was doing in Blackpool. The man replied, 'I'm spending a day with the Lord.' Fox felt that this man had been sent by God to help him, and so he told this total stranger about the emptiness of his religious search. In return the man explained, in terms that were quite new to Fox, God's plan of salvation – which he drew on a serviette!

As Fox himself later described it: 'To believe was not hard; the facts were offered to me in honest and simple truths by eye-witnesses that compelled trust. But to turn was harder. There was the risk of losing something, of surrendering my legitimate control over my own body, of yielding up my liberty. There was the challenge to change my way of life, my attitude to right and wrong. What about my money? Who would I be meant to marry? Would I have to become a missionary? These sorts of questions ... were harder.

'But what my eyes fell on, as I reflected on the literature Bernie had left me, was this verse: "But God shows his love for us in that while we were yet sinners, Christ died for us." Didn't I dare to risk losing something of this life? Did this loss compare with Jesus, who gave up all, his whole life, that I might be given life? Couldn't I trust him with all my future? If not, who could I trust?

'That night I knelt down beside my hotel bed in simple response.'

Mitsuo Fuchida (Japanese airman)

Mitsuo Fuchida led the Japanese air-raid on Pearl Harbour on 7 December 1941. His spiritual pilgrimage led him through Shintoism, Buddhism, Emperor Worship and finally to Christianity.

On a journey to Tokyo to meet General MacArthur in 1949 he was given a tract called 'I Was a Prisoner of Japan'. It told the story of Jacob de Shazer, an American who had been captured in special missions behind the Japanese lines. In prison he had been given a Bible, and through reading it had come to know Jesus Christ as his own Master and Lord. After the war he had returned to Japan as a missionary to the people whom he had once fought and hated.

The story in this booklet made a deep impression on Fuchida, and he began to read the Bible carefully himself. 'One month after the tract was given to me,' he wrote, 'I read in Luke's Gospel, "Father, forgive them, for they know not what they do," and it came home to me just what the Lord Jesus Christ had done for me. No one helped me to understand it; the Holy Spirit alone made it plain.'

After his conversion he gave over the rest of his life to the service of Jesus Christ, and was eventually ordained in the Presbyterian Church. He then became an itinerant preacher in Japan, visiting towns and villages and telling people the good news about the forgiveness of Christ.

William Haslam (nineteenth-century Cornish clergyman)

After a clerical friend had challenged the genuineness of his faith, William Haslam went through a period of spiritual darkness and despair, feeling unfit even to take a service. He went to church one Sunday expecting only to read the prayer book service, and then decided he would at least make a few remarks about the Gospel passage set for the day. In his *Diary* he wrote:

So I went up into the pulpit and gave out my text. I took it from the Gospel of the day – 'What think ye of Christ?' (Matthew 22:42). As I went on to explain the passage, I saw that the Pharisees and scribes did not know that Christ was the Son of God, or that he was come to save them. They were looking for a king, the son of David, to reign over them as they were. Something was telling me, all the time, 'You are no better than the Pharisees yourself – you do not believe that He is the Son of God, and that He is come to save you, any more than they did.'

I do not remember all I said, but I felt a wonderful light and joy coming into my soul, and I was beginning to see what the Pharisees did not. Whether it was something in my words, or my manner, or my look, I know not; but all of a sudden a local preacher, who happened to be in the congregation, stood up, and putting up his arms, shouted out in Cornish manner, 'The parson is converted! The parson is converted! Hallelujah!' and in another moment his voice was lost in the shouts and praises of three or four hundred of the congregation. Instead of rebuking this extra-ordinary 'brawling', as I should have done in a former time, I joined in the outburst of praise; and to make it more orderly, I gave out the Doxology – 'Praise God, from whom all blessings flow' – and the people sang it with heart and voice, over and over again.

Glenn Hoddle (coach of the England football team)

When Glenn Hoddle was a player in the Tottenham Hotspur football team, he went to a dinner which had been arranged by the organization 'Christians in Sport', at which he sat next to the singer Cliff Richard. As a result of this dinner Glenn began to read the Bible.

Six years later he was in Israel for the England squad's warm-up preparations for the World Cup games in Mexico. They were taken to Bethlehem and saw the likely birthplace of Jesus. Until then Glenn had thought that Jesus was little more than a story. But having seen his birthplace, Glenn became convinced that Jesus had really lived on this earth.

After he returned home he started to talk to some Christians, and through reading his Bible he found that his questions about life were answered. So he committed his life to Christ.

Jerome (fourth-century Bible translator)

As a young man Jerome had one love – literature. He would have happily spent his whole life studying it. However, one night he had a dream which changed the course of his life. In this dream he was taken up to heaven and brought before God's throne. There he was told off for spending so much time in studying the pagan classics and so little time in studying Christian books. God said to him in the dream: 'You think more of Cicero than you do of Christ. You are a Ciceronian, not a Christian.'

After that dream he decided to spend his life in studying the Bible. Soon after this, in AD 382, the Pope summoned him and told him to revise some of the manuscripts of the Psalms and to translate the Bible into Latin. Jerome spent the next 22 years of his life doing this. His translation was known as the Vulgate and became the one authorized version of the Bible until the Reformation.

C. S. Lewis (scholar and writer)

C. S. Lewis was alone in his room at Magdalen College, Oxford, when he found that his thoughts kept returning to the subject of God, whom, he says, he did not want to meet. He gave in to God in 1929, when he knelt down and acknowledged that God was indeed God. He felt as if he was 'the most dejected and reluctant convert in all England'.

At this stage Lewis thought of God as being other than human, and he did not think about Jesus Christ being God incarnate. When confronted by the truth that God had become a man, Jesus, he again put up resistance.

The final step in Lewis' Christian conversion took place while he travelled on a bus to visit Whipsnade Zoo. It was a lovely sunny morning. When he left Oxford he did not believe that Jesus Christ was the Son of God. By the time he arrived at Whipsnade he did believe it. Yet Lewis recalls that he had not spent the journey deep in thought. There were no powerful emotions linked to this change of outlook. Lewis says that some people are very unemotional about some of the most important events in their lives. He says that in his conversion experience he was like a man who, after a long sleep, still lies motionless.

Martin Luther (sixteenth-century scholar, writer and Reformer)

Martin Luther sought to do penance for his sins, as his monk's training had taught him. He went without food, drink and sleep. He beat himself until he bled. One day, when he had been missing for some time, two other monks tapped on his cell door. Getting no answer, they entered to find him unconscious on the floor, his thin body covered with blood.

When Luther visited Rome he saw the Scala Sancta, representing the 28 sacred steps which Jesus had mounted to meet Pontius Pilate. Luther was overawed. Believing that, with every step he climbed, a soul would be released from Purgatory, he went on all fours, stopping to pray at each step for his deceased relatives. Now that he could release their sinful souls from torment, he even half wished that his parents were dead. Then, at the top, he turned, looked down the stairs and asked himself, 'Is it true?'

After Luther had received his doctorate he began a brilliant career as a lecturer at the University of Wittenberg in Saxony. He made everything as simple as possible so that students could grasp the most difficult Bible passages, and his lectures were the best attended in the university.

And as he taught, Luther was slowly learning the answers to all his own questions. The letters of Paul showed that God loved sinners as much as saints. His love and forgiveness could not be won or earned. God did not look for perfection but loved mankind despite its human frailties, and when Jesus Christ died on the cross, his suffering was for their sins. Luther suddenly saw God, not as a stern judge eager to punish all wrong-doers, but as the parent who loves the naughty child as much as the good one. So Luther found inner peace with God for himself.

Steve McQueen (film star)

Steve McQueen, star of *Bullet* and many other dramatic films, tried to hide his illness from the world. He went to live, with his wife, in an isolated ranch, from which visitors were banned. Slowly, people began to talk about Steve's cancer. He eventually went into hospital, and a large tumour was removed from his abdomen. He survived the operation, only to succumb to a massive fatal heart attack 24 hours later.

A little-known fact is that a few weeks before this Steve made a special request for one particular person to visit him in his hideout. Billy Graham made the trip by plane and jeep to Steve's ranch. During their conversation Steve committed his life to the Lord Jesus Christ. It was the most momentous event in his exciting life. As Billy made to leave, Steve asked a favour of the famous evangelist. Steve asked Billy for his Bible. Billy gladly gave it to Steve with a suitable inscription hastily written on the flyleaf. This Bible reminded Steve about the day of his conversion and the presence of the living Christ, whom he trusted during the last days of his illness. Steve read this Bible, took it to hospital with him and treasured it.

Hugh Montefiore (Anglican bishop)

Hugh Montefiore came from a Jewish home. His parents sent him as a border to Rugby School, and he was very happy there. He knew nothing about the Christian Church, had never attended a Christian service of worship, and had never read the New Testament, except for a few sentences in Greek. Nor was he at all interested in Christianity. But his life changed one day when he was 16 years old. He later wrote: 'It happened to me about 5 p.m. one dark wintry afternoon ... alone in my study... I suddenly became aware of a figure in white whom I saw clearly in my mind's eye. I use this expression because I am pretty sure that a photograph would have showed nothing special on it.'

Hugh heard the words 'Follow me' and immediately knew that this was Jesus. Afterwards he was filled with 'overpowering joy' and knew that he had to follow those instructions. He was later ordained, and eventually became a bishop in the Church of England. At the end of his life Bishop Hugh wrote: 'Not for a moment do I think that this is a better way of becoming a Christian than any other. It was simply the way it happened to me.' He also said, 'For me the imitation of Christ is central to my discipleship.'

George Müller (nineteenth-century founder of orphanages)

Many people have heard of George Müller, the man of prayer, the man of faith; not so many have heard of George Müller, the man of drink, the man of robbery. Before he was 10 years old this Prussian boy had become a persistent thief. Even government funds, entrusted to his father, were not safe from his hands.

On the night when his mother lay dying, her 14-year-old son was reeling through the streets, drunk, and so out of control that his father no longer had any influence over him. By the age of 16 he was an inveterate drunk, a constant companion of convicted criminals and an ex-prisoner himself.

But George Müller had a growing sense of his sin and guilt. The turning point in his life came one Saturday evening in November 1825, when he was 21 years old. He found himself in strange company in the house of a certain Mr Wagner, where the guests all sat down and sang a hymn. As if that was not bad enough, a man then proceeded to kneel down and pray aloud, asking God to bless the meeting. This made a deep impression on George. He had never before seen anyone kneel down to pray, since it was the Prussian custom to pray standing up.

A passage was then read from the Bible, and then someone read a printed sermon. After another hymn, the owner of the house prayed, and Müller found himself thinking: 'I am much more learned than this illiterate man, but I could not pray as well as he.' A new joy was already springing up in Müller's soul. He could not explain this, and he could not give any reason why he had felt an unaccountable desire to go to this Christian meeting in the first place. He felt a new and strange peace as he lay in bed that night.

He moved from Prussia to England. In Bristol he worked to help poor children, and became a 'father' to many thousands of them. Over 80,000 children passed through the seven day schools he ran. In just one of his orphanages 10,000 children were given shelter and a home during his lifetime.

Each day before breakfast he went into his room, knelt down and prayed the Lord's Prayer. When he reached the words, 'Give us our daily bread', he prayed more earnestly. He prayed for the money to pay the milk bill and the bread bill for his orphanages. He prayed and prayed. His biographer writes of him: 'He waited on God. He waited on God. He waited on God.'

John Newton (eighteenth-century hymn-writer)

In 1774 John Newton spent a night and a day in a storm-tossed ship with death staring him in the face. This was the moment when God spoke to his conscience, and later Newton referred to this time as his 'Great Deliverance':

I went to bed that night in my usual security and indifference; but was awakened from a sound sleep by the force of a violent sea, which broke on board us. The sea had torn away the upper timbers on one side, and made the ship a mere wreck in a few minutes. Taking in all the circumstances, it was astonishing, and almost miraculous, that any of us survived to relate the story.

We had immediate recourse to the pumps; but the water increased against all our efforts: some of us were set to bailing in another part of the vessel, that is, to lade it out with buckets and pails. I continued doing this till noon, with almost every passing wave breaking over my head; but we made ourselves fast with ropes, that we might not be washed away. Although I dreaded death now, I thought, if the Christian religion were true, I could not be forgiven.

The next day I began to pray. My prayer was like the cry of the ravens, which yet the Lord does not disdain to hear. I now began to think of that Jesus whom I had so often derided: I recollected the particulars of his life, and of his death; a death for sins not his own, but, as I remembered, for the sake of those who in their distress should put their trust in him. My companions in danger were either quite unaffected, or soon forgot it all: but it was not so with me; not that I was any wiser or better than they, but because the Lord was pleased to vouchsafe me peculiar mercy.

I had a New Testament and was struck particularly by the Prodigal, Luke chapter 15. Before we arrived in Ireland I had a satisfactory evidence in my own mind of the truth of the Gospel, as considered in itself, and its exact suitableness to answer all my needs. I saw that, by the way there pointed out, God might declare, not his mercy only, but his justice also, in the pardon of sin, on the account of the obedience and sufferings of Jesus Christ. My judgment at that time embraced the sublime doctrine of 'God manifest in the flesh, reconciling the world to himself.'

After this experience Newton became a preacher of the Gospel, and many people became Christians through his ministry. In 1764 he was ordained and became the curate at Olney in Buckinghamshire, where he wrote many of his hymns, including 'How sweet the name of Jesus sounds'. He spent the last 28 years of his life as rector of St Mary Woolnoth in London, where he died in 1807.

John Owen (seventeenth-century Puritan theologian)
For years John Owen had been under the power of religious principle, but he had not yet been borne into the region of settled peace; and at times the terrors of the Lord seemed still to compass him about.

But the time had come when the burden was to fall from Owen's shoulders; and few things in his life are more truly interesting than the means by which it was unloosed. Dr Edmund Calamy was at this time minister in Aldermanbury Chapel, and attracted multitudes by his eloquence. Owen had gone one Sabbath morning to hear the celebrated Presbyterian preacher, and much was disappointed when he saw an unknown stranger from the country enter the pulpit. His companion suggested that they should leave the chapel, and hasten to the place of worship of another celebrated preacher; but Owen's strength being already exhausted, he determined to remain.

After a prayer of simple earnestness, the text was announced in these words of Matthew 8:26, 'Why are ye fearful, O ye of little faith?' Immediately it arrested the thoughts of Owen as appropriate to his present state of mind, and he breathed an inward prayer that God would be pleased by that minister to speak to his condition. The prayer was heard, for the preacher stated and answered the very doubts that had long perplexed Owen's mind; and by the time that the discourse was ended, had succeeded in leading him forth into the sunshine of a settled peace. The most

diligent efforts were used by Owen to discover the name of the preacher who had thus been to him 'as an angel of God', but without success.
John Owen (The Works of John Owen, Vol. 1)

Joshua Poole (nineteenth-century Wesleyan evangelist)

Joshua Poole started life as a child labourer in the mines of Durham, and he grew up to be a wife-batterer and an habitual drunkard.

After years of this kind of behaviour he was sent to prison for six months for attacking his wife, and one of the prison officers spoke to him about his soul at every opportunity. One day Poole read through the whole of Psalm 51. He was reduced to fear and trembling after reading it, but he thought it was no use praying. The prison officer spoke to him about Jesus, and Poole felt for the first time the awfulness of his sins. A few days later, still tearful, Poole listened to the prison officer quoting a verse from an old hymn:

> Have you succeeded yet?
> Try, try again.
> Mercy's door is open set,
> Try, try again.

Poole recalled, 'Before he had finished the verse I found peace and entered my cell that night resting by faith in Christ my Saviour. All night I prayed, I sang and shouted for joy. The man in the next door cell heard me singing and praying and although he had not prayed since his childhood, he prayed that night. The next day, I began telling the cooks about Jesus. Some of them laughed, others jeered, but others came to me by themselves and opened their hearts to me.'

Eventually Poole was reunited with his wife, and together they toured the country as he preached the Gospel to the destitute, alcoholics, tramps and street women.

Charles Simeon (nineteenth-century Cambridge preacher)

It was but the third day after my arrival [as an undergraduate at King's College, Cambridge] that I understood I should be expected in the space of about three weeks to attend the Lord's Supper. 'What,' said I, '*must* I attend?' On being informed that I must, the thought rushed into my mind that Satan himself was as fit to attend as I; and that if I must attend, I must prepare for my attendance there. Without a moment's loss of time, I bought the *Whole Duty of Man*, the only religious book that I had ever heard of, and began to read it with great diligence; at the same time calling my ways to remembrance, and crying to God for mercy; and so earnest was I in these exercises that within the three weeks I made myself quite ill with reading, fasting, and prayer.

My distress of mind continued for about three months, and well might it have continued for years, since my sins were more in number than the hairs of my head; but God in infinite condescension began at last to smile on me, and to give me a hope of acceptance with him.

But in Passion Week, as I was reading Bishop Wilson's book on the Lord's Supper, I met with an expression to this effect – 'That the Jews knew what they did, when they transferred their sin to the head of their offering.' The thought came into my mind, What, may I transfer all my guilt to another? Has God provided an Offering for me, that I may lay my sins on His head? Then, God willing, I will not bear them on my own soul one moment longer.

Accordingly I sought to lay my sins upon the sacred head of Jesus; and on the Wednesday began to have a hope of mercy; on the Thursday that hope increased; on the Friday and Saturday it became more strong; and on the Sunday morning, Easter day, April 4, I awoke early with those words on my heart and lips, 'Jesus Christ is risen today! Hallelujah! Hallelujah!'

From that hour peace flowed in rich abundance into my soul; and at the Lord's Table in our Chapel I had the sweetest access to God through my blessed Saviour.

Charles Spurgeon (nineteenth-century preacher)

I sometimes think I might have been in darkness and despair until now had it not been for the goodness of God in sending a snowstorm, one Sunday morning, while I was going to a certain place to worship. When I could go no further, I turned down a side street, and came to a little Primitive Methodist Chapel. In that chapel there may have been a dozen or fifteen people. I had heard of the Primitive Methodists, how they sang so loudly that they made people's heads ache; but that did not matter to me. I wanted to know how I might be saved, and if they could tell me that, I did not care how much they made my head ache. The minister did not come that morning; he was snowed up, I suppose. At last, a very thin-looking man, a shoemaker, or tailor, or something of that sort, went up into the pulpit to preach. Now, it is well that preachers should be instructed, but this man was really stupid. He was obliged to stick to his text, for the simple reason that he had little else to say. The text was, 'Look unto me, and be ye saved, all the ends of the earth.'

He did not even pronounce the words correctly, but that did not matter. There was, I thought, a glimpse of hope for me in that text. The preacher began thus: 'My dear friends, this is a very simple text indeed. It says, "Look". Now lookin' don't take a deal of pain. It ain't liftin' your foot or your finger; it is just, "Look". Well, a person needn't go to college to learn to look. You may be the biggest fool, and yet you can look. A person needn't be worth a thousand a year to be able to look. Anyone can look; even a child can look. But then the text says, "Look unto Me". Ay!' said he, in broad Essex, 'many of ye are lookin' to yourselves, but it's no use lookin' there. You'll never find any comfort in yourselves. Some on ye say, "We must wait for the Spirit's workin'." You have no business with that just now. Look to Christ. The text says, "Look unto Me".'

Then the good man followed up his text in this way: 'Look unto Me; I am sweatin' great drops of blood. Look unto Me; I am hangin' on the cross. Look unto Me, I am dead and buried. Look unto Me, I am sittin' at the Father's right hand. O poor sinner, look unto Me! Look unto Me!'

When he had gone on in this way and had managed to spin out ten minutes or so, he was at the end of all his tether. Then he looked at me under the gallery, and I dare-say, with so few present, he knew me to be a stranger. Just fixing his eyes on me, as if he knew all my heart, he said, 'Young man, you look very miserable.' Well, I did, but I had not been accustomed to have remarks made from the pulpit on my personal appearance before. However, it was a good blow, and it struck right home. He continued, 'and you always will be miserable – miserable in life and miserable in death – if you don't obey my text; but if you obey now, this moment you will be saved.' Then lifting up his hands, he shouted, as only a Primitive Methodist could do, 'Young man, look to Jesus Christ. Look! Look! Look! You have nothing to do but to look and live.'

I saw at once the way of salvation. I knew not what else he said – I did not take much notice of it – I was so possessed with that one thought. Like as when the bronze serpent was lifted up, the people only looked and were healed, so it was with me. I had been waiting to do fifty things, but when I heard that word, 'Look!' what a charming word it seemed to me! Oh! I looked until I could almost have looked my eyes away. There and then the cloud was gone, the darkness had rolled away, and that moment I saw the sun; and I could have risen that instant, and sung with the most enthusiastic of them, about the precious death of Christ, and the simple faith which looks alone to him.

Oh, that somebody had told me this before, 'Trust Christ, and you shall be saved.'

Leo Tolstoy

Five years ago I came to believe in Christ's teaching, and my life suddenly changed: I ceased to desire what I had previously desired, and began to desire what I formerly did not want. What had previously seemed good to me seemed evil, and what had seemed evil seemed good. It happened to me as it happens to anyone who goes out on some business and on the way suddenly decided that the business is unnecessary, and returns home. All that was on his right is now on his left, and all that was on his left is now on his right; his former wish to get as far as possible from home has changed into a wish to be as near as possible to it. The direction of my life and my desires became different, and good and evil changed places.

Augustus Toplady (nineteenth-century hymn-writer)

Augustus Toplady, who became famous as the author of the hymn, 'Rock of Ages, cleft for me', was converted in a barn at the age of 16. He later wrote about this experience: 'I shall remember that day to all eternity.' A Wesleyan evangelist named James Morris was preaching on Ephesians 2:13: 'But now in Christ Jesus you who once were far away have been brought near through the blood of Christ.' After his conversion Toplady resolved to become a clergyman and to preach the Gospel.

He was ordained at the age of 22, and his faithful and passionate preaching of the Gospel drew large crowds in Devon, where he later became the vicar of Broadhembury.

Jim Vaus

The story of Jim Vaus is one of a turn-around from self-centredness to unselfish service. A notorious criminal phone-tapper in America, Vaus was converted at one of Billy Graham's evangelistic crusades.

After he had begun to follow Christ, Vaus was approached by a man who offered him a $10,000 bribe if he would give false testimony in a libel case. Vaus said to the man, 'Haven't you heard?'

'Haven't I heard what?' replied the man.

'Jim Vaus is dead.'

Vaus recalls that 'The man's chin dropped, his eyes bulged.' He looked at Vaus as if he had gone mad.

Vaus continued, 'That's correct. The man you are looking for, who used to tap wires, make recordings and then sell them to the highest bidder, is dead. I am a new person, because it says in the Bible, "If anyone is in Christ, that person is a new creation." '

COUNSELLING

There is a medicine in the Bible for every sin-sick soul, but every soul does not need the same medicine.

R. A. Torrey

COURAGE

Courage faces fear and thereby masters it. Cowardice represses fear and is thereby mastered by it.
Martin Luther King

Lord Shaftesbury recalled the moment when he was about to introduce in the House of Commons a Bill to control child labour: 'As I stood at the table, and just before I opened my mouth, the words of God came forcibly to my mind, "Only be strong and of good courage." '

COVETOUSNESS

Take heed and beware of covetousness ... Take heed and beware of covetousness ... Take heed and beware of covetousness ... What if I should say nothing else these three or four hours?
Hugh Latimer (preaching before King Edward VI)

CREATION

Just before Charles Darwin published his book *On the Origin of Species*, Dr John Lightfoot, Vice-Chancellor of Cambridge University, had declared: 'Heaven and earth were created all together in the same instant, on October 23, 4004, BC at one in the morning.'

CRITICISM

Search others for their virtues, yourself for faults.
Author unknown

Once upon a time when Prometheus made people, he hung two bags around their necks. One bag hung down in front of them, and was full of other people's defects, and one bag hung down behind them, and was full of their own faults. In this way people could see other people's faults as large as life, but could never observe their own faults.

Moral: This story illustrates the busybody who is blind to his own faults, but always concerns himself about other people's faults.
One of Aesop's fables

CROSS OF JESUS
See also **Gardens; Heresy; Ransom; Redemption; Success; Trees**
The cross is a tree set on fire with invisible flame, that illumineth all the world. The flame is love.
Thomas Traherne

While Handel was composing the oratorio of *The Messiah*, one day he was found sobbing uncontrollably. In front of him lay the score, open at the page where these words were written: 'He was despised, He was rejected.'

There are some sciences that may be learned by the head, but the science of Christ crucified can only be learned by the heart.
C. H. Spurgeon

When I survey the wondrous cross,
On which the Prince of Glory died,
My richest gain I count but loss,
And pour contempt on all my pride.

Matthew Arnold thought that this was the finest hymn in the English language. John Julian, the author of the massive *Dictionary of Hymnology*, rates it as 'one of the four [hymns] which stand at the head of all hymns in the English language.' Eric Routley believed it to be 'the most penetrating of all hymns, the most demanding, the most imaginative.' Isaac Watts gave it the title: 'Crucifixion to the world by the cross of Christ', basing it on Galatians 6:14.

The Methodist, Dinsdale Young, said, 'If you look critically at the wondrous cross you will see in it nothing but common wood. The cross is best discerned through penitential tears.'

In his book *The Life and Times of Jesus the Messiah* Alfred Edersheim gives this description of the physical details of Jesus' crucifixion:
First the upright wood was planted in the ground. It was not high, and probably the feet of the sufferer were not above one or two feet from the ground. Thus could the communication described in the Gospels take place between him and others; thus also might his sacred lips be moistened with the sponge attached to a short stalk of hyssop. Next the transverse

wood (*antenna*) was placed on the ground and the sufferer laid upon it, when his arms were extended, drawn up and bound to it. Then … a strong sharp nail was driven first into the right, then into the left hand (the *clavi trabales*).

Next the sufferer was drawn up by means of ropes, perhaps ladders; the transverse either bound or nailed to the upright and a rest or support for the body (the *cornu* or *sedile*) fastened on it. Lastly, the feet were extended and either one nail hammered into each or a larger piece of iron through the two. And so might the crucified hang for hours, even days, in the unutterable anguish of suffering till consciousness at last failed.

CRUELTY
See also **Refugees**

On her second visit to the Home for the Wounded at Ahwaz in Iran, the British MP Emma Nicholson saw nine-year-old Amar Kanim. During the Iran–Iraq war he had suffered third-degree burns on 45 per cent of his body area. Emma brought Amar back to England and took him to Guy's Hospital, where the doctors advised that treatment would last at least 10 years. Emma and her husband adopted Amar, and he now lives with them in their Devon farmhouse.

Horrified by Saddam Hussein's draining of 3,000 square miles of marshland in southern Iraq, which has destroyed the way of life of many thousands of Iraqi people, Emma has set up the AMAR appeal (Assisting Marsh Arabs and Refugees). In her book *Secret Society* (published in 1996) she says that as a result of AMAR's work 'Over one million miserable people in Iraq and Iran have benefited from the provision of clothing, shelter, clean water, primary health care, teaching and work.' AMAR is now also working in Lebanon, Bosnia, Palestine and northern Iraq.

CULTS
The best way to make money is to start a religion.
L. Ron Hubbard (founder of the 'Church of Scientology')

Thirty-nine members of the 'Heaven's Gate' cult were found dead in April 1997 in Rancho Santa Fe, a suburb of San Diego. In total obedience to their leader, Marshall Applewhite, they dressed in black trousers, black shirts and black shoes, took a fatal dose of apple sauce laced with phenobarbitol and lay down to die. All their possessions were arranged at their feet in preparation for the journey they expected to take on an alien spaceship which they believed was travelling in the wake of the Hale-Bopp comet.

The Jehovah's Witnesses have been called the most missionary minded of all the religious sects. Every member is thought of as a minister. Nobody can become a full member unless they are engaged in regular house-to-house visiting. They have to submit reports on their visits to their local Kingdom Hall. Each Witness, on top of his or her normal work, is expected to put in at least 10 hours visiting every month and to distribute at least 12 copies of *The Watchtower* or *Awake* each week. The best Witnesses are encouraged to become Pioneers. They have to continue to support themselves by taking a part-time job, while they put in 100 hours of door-to-door visiting per month.

Some of the Pioneers become Special Pioneers. In return for a tiny allowance they become full-time Witnesses and have to spend over 140 hours a month visiting. A number of Witnesses, especially those between the ages of 20 and 26, give over two years of their lives and work full time for the movement.

D

DEATH

See also **Dying**

While I thought I was learning how to live, I have been learning how to die.
Leonardo da Vinci

Day by day remind yourself that you are going to die.
St Benedict

'To die will be an awfully big adventure.'
J. M. Barrie (Peter Pan)

Our attitude to all men would be Christian if we regarded them as though they were dying, and determined our relation to them in the light of death, both of their death and of our own.
Nicolas Berdyaev

Shih Huang Ti, the emperor of China (c. 259–210 BC), dreaded dying. Soon after he became emperor 700,000 people were forced to start building his tomb. By the time he died 6,000 life-size pottery soldiers had been made to guard the entrance to his tomb.

'It's not that I'm afraid to die. I just don't want to be there when it happens.'
Woody Allen

I die before my time; and my body will be given back to earth, to become the food of worms. Such is the fate which so soon awaits the great Napoleon.
Napoleon

DEDICATION

See also **Work**

It took computers 800,000 hours to make Walt Disney's film *Toy Story*. The mouth of the character Woody had 58 different variations.

Val Kilmer has starred in several highly successful films, including the western *Tombstone* (1993), *Batman Forever* (1995) and *The Saint* (1997). He received critical acclaim for his portrayal of the pop star Jim Morrison in Oliver Stone's *The Doors* (1991). To prepare for that role Kilmer spent all his waking hours for six months in boots and leather. He grew his hair out and lost weight. He memorized the words of every song that the pop group The Doors had ever recorded. After he had landed the part, he made a demo tape to convince Oliver Stone that he should sing the songs as well.

Fred Zinnemann, director of *High Noon, From Here to Eternity, Oklahoma, A Man for all Seasons* and *The Day of the Jackal*, died in April 1997, aged 89. He had enjoyed amazing commercial success in his film-making career, and he believed that this was because he had stuck faithfully to his own artistic principles. He said, 'One must follow one's own line, be true to the way one sees things, and trust that this will transcend passing fashion. The trust may be misplaced, but it is all one has.'

DEMON POSSESSION

In his *Dialogues*, Gregory, a sixth-century bishop of Tours, gives this account of demon possession:

Eleutherius, abbot of St Mark's monastery, lived with me for a long time in my monastery at Rome and died there. His disciples say that he raised a dead person to life by the power of prayer. He was well known for his simplicity and compunction of heart, and undoubtedly through his tears this humble, childlike soul obtained many favours from almighty God.

I will tell you about a miracle of his which I had him describe to me in his own simple words. Once while he was travelling, evening came on before he could find a lodging for the night, so he stopped at a convent. There was a little boy in this convent who was troubled every night by an evil spirit. So, after welcoming the man of God to their convent, the nuns asked him to keep the boy with him that night. He agreed, and allowed the boy to rest near him. In the morning the nuns asked him with deep concern whether he had done anything for the boy. Rather surprised that they should ask, he said, 'No'. Then they acquainted him with the boy's condition, informing him that not a night passed without the evil spirit troubling the boy. Would Eleutherius please take him along to the monastery because they could no longer bear to see him suffer. The man of God agreed to do so.

The boy remained a long time in the monastery without being troubled in the least. Highly pleased at this, the old abbot allowed his joy at the boy's healthy condition to exceed moderation. 'Brothers,' he said to the monks, 'the Devil had his joke with the sisters, but once he encountered real servants of God, he no longer dared to come near the boy.' That very instant, hardly waiting for Eleutherius to finish speaking, the Devil again took possession of the young boy, tormenting him in the presence of all. The sight of it filled the old man's heart with grief, and when his monks tried to console him he said, 'Upon my word! Not one of you shall taste bread today until this boy is snatched out of the Devil's power.'

He prostrated himself in prayer with all his monks and continued praying until the boy was freed from the power of the evil spirit. The cure was complete and the Devil did not dare molest him any further.

DEPRESSION

Before [and/or after] any great achievement, some measure of depression is very usual.
C. H. Spurgeon

Some years ago, I was the subject of fearful depression of spirit. Various troublous events had happened to me; I was also unwell, and my heart sank within me. Out of the depths I was forced to cry unto the Lord. Just before I went away to Mentone for rest, I suffered greatly in body, but far more in soul, for my spirit was overwhelmed. Under this pressure, I preached a sermon from the words, 'My God, My God, why hast Thou forsaken Me?'

I was as much qualified to preach from that text as ever I expect to be; indeed, I hope that few of my brethren could have entered so deeply into those heart-breaking words. I felt to the full of my measure the horror of a soul forsaken of God. Now, that was not a desirable experience. I tremble at the bare idea of passing again through that eclipse of soul; I pray that I may never suffer in that fashion again unless the same result should hang upon it.

That night, after the service, there came into my vestry a man who was as nearly insane as he could be to be out of an asylum. His eyes seemed ready to start from his head, and he said that he should utterly have despaired if he had not heard that discourse, which had made him feel that there was one man alive who understood his feelings, and could describe his experience. I talked with him, and tried to encourage him, and asked him to come again on the Monday night, when I should have a little more time to speak with him. I saw the brother again, and I told him that I thought he was a hopeful patient, and I was glad that the word had been so suited to his case. Apparently, he put aside the comfort which I presented for his acceptance, and yet I had the consciousness upon me that the precious truth which he had heard was at work upon his mind, and that the storm of his soul would soon subside into a deep calm.

Now hear the sequel.

Last night, of all the times in the year, when, strange to say, I was preaching from the words, 'The Almighty hath vexed my soul,' after the service, in walked the self-same brother who had called on me five years before. This time, he looked as different as noonday from midnight, or as life from death. I said to him, 'I am glad to see you, for I have often thought about you, and wondered whether you were brought into perfect peace.' I told you that I went to Mentone, and my patient also went into the country, so that we had not met for five years.

To my enquiries, this brother replied, 'Yes, you said I was a hopeful patient, and I am sure you will be glad to know that I have walked in the sunlight from that day till now. Everything is changed and altered with me.'

Dear friends, as soon as I saw my poor despairing patient the first time, I blessed God that my fearful experience had prepared me to sympathize with him and guide him; but last night, when I saw him perfectly restored, my heart overflowed with gratitude to God for my former sorrowful feelings. I would go into the deeps a hundred times to cheer a downcast spirit: it is good for me to have been afflicted that I might know how to speak a word in season to one that is weary.

C. H. Spurgeon (Autobiography)

DISABILITY AND HANDICAP

Over 20 years ago Jean Vanier invited two severely handicapped people to live with him in a small house in a French village. With very little money, they shared everything together: shopping, cleaning, cooking. That was the beginning of L'Arche communities in which able-bodied people live alongside handicapped people. Today there are 106 communities world-wide.

At a meeting in London, Vanier described a young man of 26, who could do nothing for himself, and had to be fed through his stomach. The assistants who lived with him said, 'Antonio has transformed our lives. He has brought us from a world of competitiveness to a world of tenderness and mutuality.' 'He had a power of deep communion, not through the head but through the heart.'

Vanier told Ysenda Maxtone Graham, 'The real reason L'Arche has worked is the incredible beauty of people with disabilities.'
Church Times

Let there be a law that no deformed child shall be reared.
Aristotle

In 1995, when he was in his early 40s, a French journalist, Jean-Dominique Bauby, suffered a serious stroke. It left him paralysed, only able to move his left eye-lid. He devised a way of communicating through blinking and dictated a 130 page book called *The Diving Suit and the Butterfly.* He died a few days after the book's publication.
The Week

Mad dogs we knock on the head; the fierce and savage ox we slay; sickly sheep we put to the knife and keep them from infecting the flock; unnatural progeny we destroy; we drown even children who at birth are weakly and abnormal.
Seneca

The comedian and film star Dudley Moore feels that his mother rejected him, as he was born with a club foot and a withered leg. He can never recall being hugged or kissed by his mother who, he says, even felt like killing him at birth. At school, his disability led to a great deal of teasing by the other boys, who copied his limp and called him 'Hopalong!'

DISCIPLESHIP
See also **Martyrdom**
Dietrich Bonhoeffer was born on 4 February 1906 in Breslau, Germany. When he was 17 he went to Tübingen University to study theology. He immersed himself in his studies, proving to be an independent and original thinker. His ambition was to lecture in theology at the university. Politics did not interest him. As a good Lutheran he believed it was his duty to support the State, but, step by step, in obedience to Christ, he was led to resist the growing evil of Nazism, until he was

thrown into prison and killed only three weeks before Hitler himself committed suicide.

When he was 24 Bonhoeffer went to America for a year to study at Union Theological Seminary in New York. He taught at a Sunday school and gave Bible classes in Harlem. Among these black Christians he found fellowship in Christ – a true Christian community of faith and love. For the first time, too, he experienced the horror of racial hatred.

Returning to Germany, he was ordained and became a student pastor and lecturer at the university of Berlin. The students and lecturers there were impassioned Nazis, but Bonhoeffer lectured on the evils of war.

On 30 January 1933 Hitler became Chancellor of Germany. That spring the first anti-Jewish laws were announced. To a congregation of Lutheran pastors Bonhoeffer said that the Church must oppose the State when it made wrong judgements. If a car, he said, were driven by a mad driver and went out of control, then it was not enough to bind up the wounds of injured people. A spoke must be put in the wheels. Many of his congregation walked out in disgust at his words.

In 1933 German support for Hitler reached fever pitch. Protestants who would not support Hitler joined together to form the Confessing Church. In 1935 Bonhoeffer became head of its theological seminary at Finkenwalde. Bonhoeffer's anti-Nazi views became well known. He lost his job at Berlin University, and in 1937 the seminary was closed down. Bonhoeffer wrote articles condemning government policies.

In 1939, as warfare mounted, Bonhoeffer found himself in a dilemma. He was a pacifist. All war was abhorrent to him. It was impossible for him to fight for Germany. But to refuse the call-up would endanger his friends in the Confessing Church. Unable to make a decision, he sailed for America, where his friends hoped he would stay till peace returned. However, after a very short time he returned, determined to do all he could to rid Germany of Hitler.

In 1940 he was forbidden to preach or publish. He began to work as a German double agent. He travelled in Europe, ostensibly for the Church on ecumenical missions. In reality, while pretending to find out allied military secrets, he was working with a group of conspirators who were seeking to destroy Hitler. He helped Jewish refugees to escape from Germany. In the winter of 1942–3 two assassination attempts failed. During this time Bonhoeffer tried to enlist the help of the British Government in the plot to remove Hitler.

When Bonhoeffer was eventually arrested in 1943 it was for his involvement in smuggling 14 Jews out of Germany. He was at first thrown into Tegel prison. Here, for the first 12 days, he was allowed visits from his family, and he was also allowed to read and write letters. He hid his connection with the conspirators, whilst still communicating to them in code. Bonhoeffer spent 18 months in Tegel prison, where he wrote his *Letters and Papers from Prison*, one of the classics of twentieth-century Christian literature.

One year after his arrest, no evidence having been found to implicate him in the conspiracy, the charge was dropped. Whilst he was at Tegel he was given the opportunity to escape, with the help of the guards. However, he refused to run away because this would have put his uncle and brother – fellow prisoners – in danger. In July 1944 the assassination plot was discovered and the conspirators were executed. On 23 August he wrote: 'You must never doubt that I'm travelling with gratitude and cheerfulness along the road where I'm being led. My past life is brim full of God's goodness, and my sins are covered by the forgiving love of Christ crucified.'

In October 1944 a secret file was discovered which revealed that Bonhoeffer had been working with the anti-Hitler conspirators for many years. He was moved to the Gestapo prison in Prinz-Albrecht Strasse. Here he was brutally tortured but remained unbroken, calm, cheerful and trusting. On 7 February 1945 he was transferred to Buchenwald, where he was kept in the cellar of a house outside the main concentration camp. A British officer, imprisoned at Buchenwald, wrote:

Bonhoeffer was different; just quiet, calm and normal, seemingly perfectly at his ease. His soul really shone in the dark desperation of our prison. He was all humility and sweetness. He was one of the very few men I have ever met to whom his God was real and close to him.

The war was now drawing to a close. The prisoners could hear American guns and expected to be released. Then, after seven weeks, Bonhoeffer was taken to the village of Schönberg and was kept in the school there. But then some documents were found which clearly implicated him in the conspiracy. On 8 April the SS arrived. 'Prisoner Bonhoeffer, get ready and come with us,' they said. Bonhoeffer asked an Englishman, Payne Best, to give a message to Bishop Bell of Chichester: 'Tell him that for me this is the end but also the beginning.' The prison doctor witnessed Bonhoeffer's death the following day:

Through the half-open door in one room of the huts I saw Pastor Bonhoeffer, before taking off his prison garb, kneeling on the floor praying fervently to his God. I was most deeply moved by the way this lovable man prayed, so devout and so certain that God heard his prayer. At the place of execution, he again said a short prayer and then climbed the steps to the gallows, brave and composed. His death ensued after a few seconds. In almost fifty years that I worked as a doctor, I have hardly ever seen a man die so entirely submissive to the will of God.

When Christ calls a man he bids him come and die.
Dietrich Bonhoeffer

DISCIPLINE
See also **Children**

A schoolboy stole his classmate's books and took them to his mother. The mother, instead of reproving him, praised him. On another occasion he brought his mother a coat he had stolen, for which he was praised even more highly. When he grew up he embarked on many more serious thefts, until one day he was caught in the act of stealing. His hands were tied behind his back and he was led away to be executed.

His mother went to him, beating her breast, and her son said that he wanted to whisper something in her ear. As soon as she went close to him he bit off her ear-lobe with his teeth. The mother told him off for behaving in such a terrible way towards her. Not satisfied with all his other crimes, he now committed grievous bodily harm against his mother.

'The time when you should have reproved me,' replied the son, 'was when I committed my first theft, when I brought you the books I stole as a schoolboy. If you had done that I would not have ended up in the hands of the executioner.'

Moral: Offenders go from bad to worse if they are not checked.
One of Aesop's fables

DISCOVERIES
See also **Science**

Archimedes of Syracuse, the greatest mathematician and engineer of the third century BC, was given a problem to solve. The philosopher Hiero, King of Syracuse, told him that he wanted to know if the crown that had been made for him by the local goldsmith was made of solid gold, or gold alloy or just a gold-coloured metal. Archimedes thought about this for days. Wherever he went he was trying to think of a way to solve this problem for his king. He was still thinking about it when he went to the public baths and let himself into the water.

As he lowered himself into the bath he observed that the water level rose. He then let out a loud shout, 'Eureka!' (meaning, 'I have found the solution'). After making this discovery he went on to formulate the proposition that a solid plunged into a fluid loses an amount of weight equal to the volume of the displaced water. Now he could help the king to discover if his crown was pure gold. When he let out his cry of 'Eureka!' he was expressing the excitement of making a scientific discovery.

When the first Christians, such as Andrew, Simon, John and James, met Jesus, they made the discovery that he was the world's Saviour and their Saviour. When Andrew said, 'We have found the Messiah', he used the same Greek word meaning 'found' that Archimedes had used for his discovery.

DOUBT

It is not as a child that I believe and confess Christ. My hosanna is born of a furnace of doubt.

Fyodor Dostoevsky

DREAMS

Born in 1889 in the North Indian state of Patiala, the Christian preacher Sundar Singh was most influenced in his early life by his Sikh mother. Once a week he was taken to sit at the feet of a Sikh sadhu who lived some miles from his home in the middle of a jungle. But Sundar Singh was blessed enough to be sent to a Christian mission school. His mother hoped he would learn English, but he also learned about Jesus Christ and his love for everyone in the world.

When Sundar Singh was 14 years old his mother died, and he was deeply distressed. He took it out on the missionaries who ran the school, making fun of their converts. He then burned a Bible, one page at a time, at his home. That night he went to bed planning to take his own life the following day on the railway line.

But before it was light he woke his father and told him that he had had a vision during the night in which he had seen Jesus Christ and had heard his voice. He told his father that he would spend his life following Christ.

Sundar Singh's father tried to persuade him to renounce his conversion, and he even attempted to poison his son when he refused to do so. Sundar Singh spent the remaining 25 years of his life witnessing to Jesus, in the teeth of fierce opposition.

DUTY

'England expects that every man will do his duty.' Admiral Horatio Nelson signalled this message to the British fleet at 11.30 a.m. on 21 October 1805. The Spanish and French fleets were in sight, and the Battle of Trafalgar was just about to begin. Nelson said to one of his captains, 'I will now amuse the fleet with a signal. Send: "Nelson confides that every man will do his duty." ' It was pointed out to him that 'England' would be an improvement on 'Nelson', and Flag Lieutenant Pasco told Nelson that whereas 'confides' was not in the signal book and would therefore take seven flags to communicate, the word 'expects' was in the signal book. So the famous message read, 'England expects that every man will do his duty.'

When one admiral, Lord Collingwood, saw this message coming from HMS *Victory*, he said, 'I wish Nelson would stop signalling, as we all know well enough what we have to do.'

DYING
See also **Death**

David Watson

In November 1983 the preacher and writer David Watson already knew that he had cancer, but he carried on with a major mission in Dublin and Belfast which had been booked up for months. As Christians became aware of the seriousness of his illness, they prayed. Surely this faithful preacher of the Gospel would be healed? At one point it seemed that there was a remission.

In the epilogue of *Fear No Evil*, the last book he wrote, Watson reveals how he faced up to death: 'Whatever else is happening to me physically, God is working deeply in my life. In that position of security I have experienced once again his perfect love, a love that casts out fear.'

David Watson died on Saturday 18 February 1984. At his thanksgiving service the Archbishop of Canterbury said in his sermon: 'He was a burning and shining light. He was for the church, and for the world and for people. He stood as a lamp on a lamp-stand, for the illumination of the world. Perhaps his greatest resource was that he knew that he would go to his eternal home and find his Father waiting for him.'

Sir Walter Scott

On July 11th, 1832, Sir Walter Scott arrived at Abbotsford after a long and trying journey from London. The next morning, he was wheeled up and down the garden where the lawns and roses were in their full summer beauty.

On the 13th, after an hour or two in the garden, he was taken into the library. His chair was placed beside the great central window so that he could look down towards the Tweed. He asked his son-in-law to read to him.

Lockhart glanced at the shelves loaded with books. Was he thinking of some earlier favourite? Did he perhaps have one of his own books in mind? Lockhart ventured to ask which book he should read from. Like a flash, back came the reply: 'Need you ask? There is but one.' And Lockhart understood at once; he opened the Bible and began to read from the fourteenth chapter of St John: 'Let not your heart be troubled; ye believe in God, believe also in me. In my Father's house are many mansions: if it were not so I would have told you. I go to prepare a place for you.' Sir Walter Scott murmured: 'This is great comfort.'

Two days later, Lockhart read to him once more from the New Testament and he followed it all with great comfort. But he declined very quickly and his mind grew clouded. The few words that others could catch were fragments of Scripture. It was on September 21st that he breathed his last.

'It was a beautiful day,' Lockhart wrote, 'so warm that every window was open, and so perfectly still that the sound of all others most delicious to his ear, the gentle ripple of the Tweed over its pebbles, was distinctly audible as we knelt around his bed.'

But the sound was not so lovely nor so full of comfort as the words from St John's Gospel which had soothed the dying man's mind.
J. G. Lockhart

Mr Valiant-for-Truth

Mr Valiant-for-Truth said 'I am going to my Father's; and though with great difficulty I have got hither, yet now I do not repent me of all the trouble I have been at to arrive where I am... My marks and scars I carry with me, to be a witness for me that I have fought his battles, who now will be my rewarder.'

When the day that he must go hence was come, many accompanied him to the river-side; into which, as he went, he said, 'Death, where is thy sting?' And as he went deeper he said, 'Grave, where is thy victory?' So he passed over, and all the trumpets sounded for him on the other side.
John Bunyan (Pilgrim's Progress)

A dying student

Martin Luther once visited a student whom he knew was dying. Luther asked the young man what he would like to take to God, in whose presence he would shortly appear. The man replied, 'Everything that is good, sir.'

Luther was surprised, and said, 'Why do you say that, as you are only a poor sinner?'

The young man replied, 'I will take to God in heaven a penitent, humble heart sprinkled with the blood of Christ.'

I am so weak that I can hardly write, I cannot read my Bible, I cannot even pray. I can only lie still in God's arms like a little child, and trust.
Hudson Taylor (during his final days)

EDUCATION

Educate men without religion and you make them but clever devils.
Duke of Wellington

ENDURANCE

George Matheson, a Scottish minister, suffered some great sadnesses in his life. He lost his sight and his fiancée broke off their engagement. In a prayer he wrote he asks that he might accept God's will, 'not with dumb resignation, but with holy joy; not only with the absence of murmur, but with a song of praise.' Christian endurance enables a person to do that.

EQUALITY

See also **Inequality**
All men are created equal.
Thomas Jefferson (Preamble to the American Declaration of Independence, 1776)

ETERNAL LIFE

Long ago the Greeks saw that a life that simply went on for ever would not necessarily be a blessing. They told the story of Aurora, the goddess of dawn, who fell in love with Tithonus, the god of mortal youth. Zeus offered Aurora any gift she might choose for her mortal lover. She asked that Tithonus might never die; but she forgot to ask that he might remain for ever young. So Tithonus lived for ever, growing older and more and more decrepit, till life became a terrible and intolerable curse.

Life is only of value when it is nothing less than the life of God – and this is the meaning of eternal life.

ETERNITY

Over the magnificent triple doorway of Milan Cathedral are three inscriptions. Above one is carved a wreath of roses, with the words, 'All that pleases is but for a moment.' Over the second is a cross, with the words, 'All that troubles is but for a moment.' Over the great central entrance to the main aisle is inscribed: 'That only is important which is eternal.'

EVANGELISM
See also **Conversion**

Why does the church exist?
The church exists for those outside it.
William Temple

Archbishop William Temple described bringing someone to Jesus as 'the greatest service that one person can do another'.

This has been called the clearest statement in the New Testament on how to become a Christian: 'To all who received him, to those who believed in his name, he gave the right to become children of God' (John 1:12). There are three crucial verbs in the sentence: *receive, believe* and *become*. In becoming a Christian there is something to be believed and someone to be received.

In St Paul's Cathedral and in the Chapel at Keble College, Oxford, there are two famous, almost identical paintings, by Holman Hunt. They depict Jesus Christ as *The Light of the World*. On 5 May 1854 John Ruskin wrote to *The Times* with this description of the paintings:

The inscription beneath the painting is the beautiful verse: 'Behold I stand at the door and knock. If anyone hears my voice and opens the door, I will come in to him and sup with him, and he with me' (Revelation 3:20). On the left hand side of the picture is seen this door of the human soul. It is fast barred; its bars and nails are rusty, it is knitted and bound to its doorpost by creeping tendrils of ivy, showing that it has never been opened. Christ approaches it in the night time.

In this picture Jesus Christ, the Saviour of the world, stands knocking at the door of the human heart, waiting for an invitation to be offered so that he can come in.

There are numerous significant details in this painting. There is no handle on the outside of the door. The painter explained, 'Its only handle is on the inside', emphasizing the point that Christ never barges his way into anyone's life, but patiently waits to be invited in.

Christ's feet are pointing down the road, as if he does not expect anyone to open the door to him, and he is about to pass on to the next house. Hunt wrote some words on the canvas which are not visible today, as they are covered by the frame at the bottom of the picture. The words are *Nec me praetermittas, domine* ('Neither pass me by, Lord').

On one occasion the writer Rudyard Kipling told William Booth, the founder of the Salvation Army, that he disliked tambourines. 'Young man,' replied Booth, 'if I thought I could win one more soul for Christ by standing on my head and beating a tambourine with my feet I would learn how to do it.'

I had never lost sight of Jesus Christ since the first night I met him in the store in Boston. But for years I was only a nominal Christian, really believing that I could not work for God. No one had ever asked me to do anything. When I went to Chicago I hired five pews in a church, and used to go out on the street and urge young men to fill the pews. I never spoke to those young men about their souls; that was the work of elders, I thought. After working for some time like that, I started a mission Sunday School. I thought numbers were everything, and so I worked for numbers. When the attendance fell below one thousand, it troubled me; and when it went up to over fifteen hundred, I was elated. Still, nobody was converted; there was no harvest. Then God opened my eyes.

There was a class of young ladies in the Sunday School who were without exception the most frivolous set of girls I ever met. One Sunday the teacher was ill and I took the class. They laughed in my face and I felt like opening the door and telling them all to get out and never come back. That week the teacher of the class visited me in the store where I worked. He was pale and looked very ill. 'What's the trouble?' I asked. 'I've had another haemorrhage in my lungs. The doctor says I cannot live on Lake Michigan, so I am going to New York State. I suppose I am going home to die.' He seemed very upset and when I asked why, he replied, 'Well, I have never led any of my class to Christ. I really believe that I have done the girls more harm than good.'

I had never heard anyone talk like that before and it set me thinking. After a while I said, 'Suppose you go and tell them how you feel. I will go with you in a carriage, if you want to go.' He agreed and we set off together. It was one of the best journeys I ever had on earth. We went to the house of one of the girls, called for her, and the teacher talked to her about her soul. There was no laughing then! Before long, tears stood in her eyes. After he explained how Jesus could be her own Saviour he suggested that we prayed. He asked me to pray. I had never done such a thing. I prayed to God to convert a young lady there and then. God answered our prayers.

We went to other houses. He went up the stairs, became very breathless, and told the girls why he had come. It wasn't long before they broke down and asked for God's salvation. When he became exhausted, I took him back to his home. The following day we went out again. At the end of ten days he came to the store with his face literally shining. 'Mr Moody,' he said, 'the last one of my class has given herself to Christ.' We had a great time of rejoicing.

He had to leave the following night, so I called his class together that night for a prayer meeting, and there God lit a fire in my soul that has never gone out. My great ambition had been to be a successful merchant, and if I had known that meeting was going to remove that ambition from me, I might not have gone. But how many times since then have I thanked God for that meeting.

The dying teacher sat in the middle of his class and told them to read John chapter fourteen. We sang a chorus and then prayed. I was getting up from my knees when one of the members of the class began to pray for her dying teacher. Another prayed, and another, and before we rose the whole class had prayed. As I went out I said to myself, 'Oh, God, let me die rather than lose the blessing I have received this night.' I didn't know what this was going to cost me. I was disqualified for business; it had become distasteful to me. I got a taste for another world, and no longer cared about making money. Over the next few days a great struggle took place in my life. Should I give up business and give myself to Christian work or should I not? I have never regretted the choice. Oh, the privilege of leading someone out of the darkness of this world into the glorious light and freedom of the Gospel.
D. L. Moody

> We are the Bibles the world is reading;
> We are the creeds the world is needing;
> We are the sermons the world is heeding.
Billy Graham

One is Christianized to the extent that he is a Christianizer. One is evangelized to the extent that he is an evangelist.
Léon Joseph (Belgian archbishop)

Go for souls, and go for the worst.
William Booth's motto

The following Christian leaders gave their hearts to Jesus Christ in their childhood: Polycarp (aged nine); Matthew Henry (eleven); Jonathan Edwards (seven); and Isaac Watts (nine).

In a journal called *The Type Speaks* the typographer F. W. Goudy (1865–1947) wrote, 'I am: the leaden army that conquers the world – I am TYPE.' Another version of this saying is, 'With twenty-six lead soldiers [i.e. the characters of the alphabet set up for printing] I can conquer the world.'

There's a story about a famous preacher, Dr Graham Scroggie, who worked in England over 50 years ago. One night he had been speaking to a big audience in a huge tent on the subject of the lordship of Christ. At the end of his sermon the crowd of people left, all except for one college student. She stayed behind, all alone, in her seat. Scroggie went over to her and gently asked if there was any way in which he could help her. 'Dr Scroggie,' she blurted out, 'your message was so compelling. But I'm scared to make Jesus Christ my Lord. I'm afraid about what he may ask of me!'

Scroggie turned the worn pages of his old Bible to the place where Peter had a vision in Joppa. In Peter's trance he saw a large sheet being let down to earth by its four corners. On it were all kinds of animals which orthodox Jews considered to be unclean. Then a voice said, 'Get up, Peter. Kill and eat.' Three times Peter replied, 'No, Lord.' Then the elderly preacher explained to the young student: 'You can say, "No", and you can say, "Lord", but you can't really say, "No, Lord." I'm going to leave a pen with you while I go outside to pray for you. Here's a piece of paper. I'm writing these two words on it: "Lord"; "No". You can cross out whichever word you like.'

Scroggie returned ten minutes later to find the student in floods of tears. He could see that the word 'No' had been crossed out on the piece of paper. He could just make out the words which the student uttered, in a low whisper: 'He's Lord. He's Lord. He's Lord.'

EVIL

See also **Temptation**

It is men, not God, who have produced racks, whips, prisons, slavery, guns, bayonets, and bombs; it is by human avarice or human stupidity, not by the churlishness of nature, that we have poverty and overwork.
C. S. Lewis

EXAMPLE

Example is not the main thing in influencing others. It is the only thing.
Albert Schweitzer

EXPERIENCES OF GOD
See also **Conversion**

Thomas Aquinas (medieval philosopher)
Towards the end of his life Thomas Aquinas had a mystical experience that moved him so much that he never wrote or dictated another word, even though he had spent a great deal of his life writing numerous books. One of his secretaries tried to encourage him to start writing again, but he replied, 'I am unable to do that. Everything that I have written now seems to me to be like straw, in comparison with what I have seen and what has been revealed to me.'

Jonathan Edwards (eighteenth-century preacher)
Jonathan Edwards was converted when he was nearly 18. His conversion story ranks with those of people like Augustine and Pascal, whose experience of the risen Christ was beyond words. Here is Edwards' own stumbling attempt to express the inexpressible:

A calm, sweet Abstraction of the Soul from all concerns of this world; and a kind of vision, or fix'd ideas and imaginations, of being alone in the mountains, or some solitary wilderness, far from all mankind; sweetly conversing with Christ, and wrapt and swallowed up in God. The sense I had of divine things would often of a sudden as it were, kindle up a sweet burning in my heart; an ardour of my soul, that I know not how to express.

At about this time Edwards read 1 Timothy 1:17: 'Now to the King eternal, immortal, invisible, the only God, be honour and glory for ever and ever. Amen.' After he had read this scripture he had another experience of Christ:

There came into my soul, and was as if it were diffused through it, a sense of the glory of the divine being; a new sense, quite different from anything I had experienced before. From about that time I began to have a new kind of apprehension and idea of Christ, and the work of redemption, and the glorious way of salvation by him.

Jonathan Edwards' wife
Last night was the sweetest night I ever had in my life. I never before, for so long a time together, enjoyed so much of the light and rest and sweetness of heaven in my soul, but without the least agitation of body during the whole time. Part of the night I lay awake, sometimes asleep, and sometimes between sleeping and waking. But all night I continued in a

constant, clear, and lively sense of the heavenly sweetness of Christ's excellent love, of his nearness to me, and of my dearness to him; with an inexpressibly sweet calmness of soul in an entire rest in him. I seemed to myself to perceive a glow of divine love come down from the heart of Christ in heaven into my heart in a constant stream, like a stream or pencil of sweet light.

At the same time my heart and soul all flowed out in love to Christ, so that there seemed to be a constant flowing and reflowing of heavenly love, and I appeared to myself to float or swim, in these bright, sweet beams, like the motes swimming in the beams of the sun, or the streams of his light which come in at the window. I think that what I felt each minute was worth more than all the outward comfort and pleasure which I had enjoyed in my whole life put together. It was pleasure, without the least sting, or any interruption. It was a sweetness, which my soul was lost in; it seemed to be all that my feeble frame could sustain.

There was but little difference, the sweetness was greatest while I was asleep. As I awoke early the next morning, it seemed to me that I had no more to do with any outward interest of my own than with that of a person whom I never saw. The glory of God seemed to swallow up every wish and desire of my heart. And it seemed to me that I found a perfect willingness, quietness, and alacrity of soul in consenting that it should be so, if it were most for the glory of God, so that there was no hesitation, doubt, or darkness in my mind. The glory of God seemed to overcome me and swallow me up, and every conceivable suffering, and everything that was terrible to my nature, seemed to shrink to nothing before it. This resignation continued in its clearness and brightness the rest of the night, and all the next day and the night following, and on Monday in the forenoon, without interruption or abatement.

D. L. Moody (nineteenth-century evangelist)

Here is Moody's account of a very special encounter with God:

I began to cry as never before, for a greater blessing from God. The hunger increased; I really felt that I did not want to live any longer. [Although he was a Christian minister and was seeing people being converted, he wanted still more people to come to Christ.] I kept on crying all the time that God would fill me with his Spirit.

Well, one day in the city of New York – oh! what a day, I cannot describe it, I seldom refer to it. It is almost too sacred an experience to name. Paul had an experience of which he never spoke for 14 years. I can only say, God revealed himself to me, and I had such an experience of his love that I had to ask him to stay his hand.

I went preaching again. The sermons were not different; I did not present any new truths, and yet hundreds were converted. I would not now be placed back where I was before that blessed experience if you should give me all the world – it would be small dust in the balance.

Martyn Lloyd-Jones, commenting on Moody's experience, wrote:

It was so overwhelming, he felt as if he was going to be physically crushed. The love of God! That is what is meant by 'the love of God in your hearts'. That is the baptism of the Spirit. That is what turned D. L. Moody from a good, regular, ordinary minister, into the evangelist who was so signally used of God in this and in other countries.

David Brainerd (evangelist to the American Indians)

In a mournful melancholy state, on July 12, 1739, I was attempting to pray; but found no heart to engage in that or any other duty; my former concern, exercise, and religious affections were now gone. I thought that the Spirit of God had quite left me; but still was not distressed; yet disconsolate, as if there was nothing in heaven or earth could make me happy. Having been thus endeavouring to pray – though, as I thought, very stupid and senseless – for near half an hour; then, as I was walking in a thick grove, unspeakable glory seemed to open to the apprehension of my soul. I do not mean any external brightness, nor any imagination of a body of light, but it was a new inward apprehension or view that I had of God, such as I never had before, nor anything which had the least resemblance to it. I had no particular apprehension of any one person in the Trinity, either the Father, the Son, or the Holy Spirit; but it appeared to be Divine glory.

My soul rejoiced with joy unspeakable, to see such a God, such a glorious Divine Being; and I was inwardly pleased and satisfied that he should be God over all for ever and ever. My soul was so captivated and delighted with the excellency of God that I was even swallowed up in him; at least to that degree that I had no thought about my own salvation, and scarce reflected that there was such a creature as myself. I continued in this state of inward joy, peace, and astonishing, till near dark without any abatement; and then began to think and examine what I had seen; and felt sweetly composed in my mind all the evening following. I felt myself in a new world, and everything about me appeared with a different aspect from what it was wont to do.

FAITH

See also **Action; Reason; Science; Work**

God does not keep an extra supply of goodness that is higher than faith, and there is no help at all in anything that is below it. *Within* faith is where the Lord wants us to stay.

Julian of Norwich (Revelations of Divine Love)

A huge crowd of people were watching the famous tightrope walker, Charles Blondin, cross over the Niagara Falls one day in 1860. He crossed over on the rope numerous times – a 1,000-foot journey, 160 feet above the raging water. He pushed a wheelbarrow with a bag of cement in it across the rope, and was cheered on reaching the other side.

The story is told that he spoke to the crowd, asking them: 'Do you believe that I can do anything on a tightrope?' 'Oh, yes, Blondin, we believe you could do anything,' they called back. Blondin approached one reporter and asked if he believed that he could take him across the Niagara Falls. The reporter said he was certain Blondin could do this. But when Blondin asked him to get into the wheelbarrow the invited man refused to go.

It is like that with Jesus Christ. Mental assent or even verbal assent is not enough. There must be trust in Christ alone.

An extended version of the Blondin story goes like this:

Eventually Blondin found a volunteer who was prepared to allow him to push him on the tightrope in a wheelbarrow across the Falls. Some of the crowd had placed bets on whether Blondin and the man in the wheelbarrow would reach the other side safely. Halfway across the 1,000-foot journey all seemed to be going very well until one man, fearful that he was about to lose the massive bet that he had placed on Blondin failing, cut a guy rope, so that the tightrope swayed dangerously. The man in the wheelbarrow was frozen with fear, knowing that Blondin and he were only moments away from a watery grave in the raging Falls. Blondin kept his head and shouted to the man, 'Stand up. Stand up and grab my shoulders.' But the man was glued to the spot in fear, gripping the sides of the wheelbarrow with all his strength. Eventually he did manage to stand up and put his hands around Blondin's neck and his legs around his waist. Blondin let the wheelbarrow fall into the turbulent water below and then allowed the tightrope to stop swaying. Very slowly, inch by inch, he then carried the man across the rope until he landed him safely on the other side.

Expect great things from God,
Attempt great things for God.
William Carey

It is the heart which is conscious of God, not the reason. This then is faith: God is sensible to the heart, not to the reason.
Blaise Pascal

Faith is the first step in understanding; understanding is the reward of faith.
Augustine

Reason is our soul's left hand,
Faith her right.
By these we reach divinity.
John Donne

FAITHFULNESS

He is invited to do great things who receives small things greatly.
Cassiodorus

I do not pray for success, I ask for faithfulness.
Mother Teresa (when asked if she was ever discouraged)

The evangelist D. L. Moody led to God a man called Mordecai Ham. Mordecai also became an evangelist, and he converted Billy Graham, who led tens of thousands of people to God.

FAMILY LIFE

See also **Children**

One of the most revolting features of the Mediterranean world into which Jesus was born was child murder. In a letter written in the reign of

Caesar Augustus a man named Hilarion advised his pregnant wife Alis to throw her baby onto the rubbish tip if she did not want it. He knew that nobody would object.

The Jews had a greater respect for children, but even they often treated their children in an overbearing way. Hence Paul's remarks in Colossians 3:21: 'Fathers, do not embitter your children, or they will become discouraged.'

With these facts in mind, it's easy to understand the disciples' astonishment when Jesus took children in his arms and blessed them. He was ushering in a new era when children would be valued, not as goods to be possessed, or as livestock to be ordered about, but for their own sake and as the heirs of the Kingdom of Heaven.

The British film actress Helena Bonham Carter, who gave up her place at Cambridge University to become an actress, lived at home until she was 30 years old because 'I love it. After I've been out, I lie on Mum's bed and tell her about it, and we'll share our days.'

I was a good provider but not a very good father, because I was away so much.
John Humphries (British broadcaster)

FASHION
The fashion wears out more apparel than the man.
William Shakespeare

FASTING
Whoso will pray, he must fast and be clean,
And fat his soul and make his body lean.
Geoffrey Chaucer ('The Summoner's Tale' in The Canterbury Tales*)*

FEAR
See also **Courage**
A man who fears suffering is already suffering from what he fears.
Michel de Montaigne

FELLOWSHIP

Wild geese can fly thousands of kilometres, across whole continents, on their migratory flights. According to Professor Margaret Kuhn, a research scientist working in this field, one thing which helps these birds on their intercontinental flights is that they rotate leadership, so that one bird does not always lead them. Another factor is that the birds behind the leader let out a 'honk' which Professor Kuhn believes to be not a cry of pain but a sound of encouragement to their leader and to each other.

Each for all and all for each.
Slogan of the Co-operative Wholesale Society

The Bible knows nothing of solitary religion.
John Wesley

FILM STARS
See also **Hollywood; Success; Tears**

FLATTERY

Flattery is a false coinage, which our vanity puts into circulation.
La Rochefoucauld

I can't be your friend, and your flatterer too.
Thomas Fuller

Flattery corrupts both the receiver and giver.
Edmund Burke

A certain fox spotted a raven in a tree with a morsel in his mouth, which started his mouth watering. The problem was how to obtain the morsel. 'Oh blessed bird,' said the fox, 'the delight of gods and men.' The fox continued to extol all the virtues of the raven, his graceful ways, his beautiful plumage and his gift of being able to predict the future. 'And now,' said the fox, 'if you had a voice to match your other excellent qualities, the sun in the heavens could not show the world a creature to match you.'

This sickly flattery immediately made the raven want to give the fox an example of his singing. But as he opened his mouth to sing he dropped his breakfast, which the fox gobbled up. The fox then told the raven to remember that whatever he had said about his beauty, he had said nothing about his brains.

One of Aesop's fables

FORGIVENESS

See also **Torture**

Once God preached to me by a similitude in the depth of winter. The earth was black, and there was scarcely a green thing or a flower to be seen. As I looked across the fields, there was nothing but barrenness – bare hedges and leafless trees, and black earth, wherever I gazed. All of a sudden God spoke, and unlocked the treasures of the snow, and the white flakes descended until there was no blackness to be seen, and all was one sheet of dazzling whiteness. At the time I was seeking the Saviour, and not long before I found Him, and I remember well that sermon which I saw before me in the snow: 'Come now, and let us reason together, saith the Lord: though your sins be as scarlet, they shall be as white as snow; though they be red like crimson, they shall be as wool.'

C. H. Spurgeon

When Christ's hands were nailed to the cross, he also nailed your sins to the cross.

Bernard of Clairvaux

Centuries ago personal bankruptcy was a very public matter. A list of all the debts of the bankrupt person was written on a parchment which was then nailed up in a public place such as the village square. There was one way that these debts could be cancelled. A friend or benefactor could remove the nail from the parchment, fold it in two and write his own name across it. Then he had to nail the folded parchment so that all could see that he had signed it and had undertaken to pay all the debts.

Two works of mercy set a man free: forgive and you will be forgiven, and give and you will receive.

Augustine

General Oglethorpe: 'I never forgive.'

John Wesley: 'Then, sir, I hope that you never sin.'

It is seldom that a person under a sentence of death has refused a pardon. Yet there is one such case on record in the annals of the US Supreme Court. Two men named Wilson and Porter had been sentenced to be hanged for robbing the US mail in 1829. Porter was executed on 2 July 1830. About three weeks before his own execution Wilson was granted a pardon by President Andrew Jackson, but he refused to accept it.

Refusal to accept a pardon was a point of law that had never been raised before, and the Supreme Court was called upon to give a decision. So in January 1833 the Court handed down the following decision, written by Chief Justice John Marshall:

A pardon is an act of grace, proceeding from the power intrusted with the execution of the laws, which exempts the individual on whom it is bestowed, from the punishment the law inflicts for a crime he has committed. A pardon is a deed, to the validity of which delivery is essential, and delivery is not complete without acceptance. It may then be rejected by the person to whom it is rendered: and if it is rejected we have found no power in a Court to force it upon him.

This was a very unusual case, and most people would agree that Wilson was a fool to refuse to accept a pardon.

In Justice Marshall's definition, 'A pardon is an act of grace' – a free, unmerited favour. It is unearned; it cannot be bought. The decision also reads, 'A pardon is a deed, to the validity of which delivery is essential, and delivery is not complete without acceptance.

Wilson's pardon cost only the scratch of the President's pen. Our pardon cost the life-blood of God's Son.

Martin Luther once had a dream in which there was a book where all his sins were written. In the dream, the devil spoke to Luther: 'Martin, here is one of your sins, here is another,' pointing to the writing in the book. Then Luther said to the devil: 'Take a pen and write, "The blood of Jesus Christ, God's Son, cleanses us from all sin." '

'I can forgive, but I cannot forget' is only another way of saying, 'I cannot forgive.'
Henry Ward Beecher

In the early 1800s Count von Massenbach, a man previously held in high esteem in Prussian society, was condemned to solitary life imprisonment in the impregnable fortress of Glatz, for high treason against King Frederick William III.

For a year Massenbach lived without hope. He was a sceptic. The only book given to him was a Bible, but he would not open it. However, he eventually began to read it, to pass the time. His heart was full of bitterness, and as he read he was angry with God for allowing him to suffer in this way. He had tried to secure his release through his influential friends, and he had even written to the king himself, but all to no avail.

One dismal November night as he lay in his cell, unable to sleep, with a terrific storm howling round the castle, his whole life of sin came before him, and he saw that his rejection of God was the root cause of all his trouble.

For the first time in his life his heart grew tender, and, opening the Bible, he read these words: 'Call upon me in the day of trouble; I will deliver you, and you will honour me.' They reached the depths of his soul, and, falling on his knees, he asked God for mercy and forgiveness, as he poured out his soul in prayer to God, asking that he might not have to spend the rest of his life in prison.

That same night the king was in his palace, unable to sleep, and in great inner turmoil. Utterly exhausted from lack of sleep, he asked God to give him one hour of refreshing sleep. This prayer was granted. Then the king said to his wife, 'God has been merciful to me, and I have reason to be grateful. Who is the man in my kingdom who has most offended me? I want to forgive him.'

'Undoubtedly, the Count von Massenbach, who is at Glatz,' answered the queen.

'You are right. I will free him.'

So, before dawn, a messenger was sent off to Glatz with a pardon for the Count, who, during that same night, had prayed earnestly for release.

'All we like sheep have gone astray; we have turned every one to his own way; and the Lord hath laid on him the iniquity of us all.' Go in at the first 'all' and come out at the last 'all'.
D. L. Moody

Only one petition in the Lord's Prayer has any condition attached to it: it is the petition for forgiveness.
William Temple

FREE WILL
We have to believe in free will. We've got no choice.
Isaac Bashevis Singer (quoted in The Times*)*

FREEDOM

The French philosopher, Jean-Jacques Rousseau, wrote in his *Social Con-tract* that 'Man is born free, but everywhere he is in chains.' Maximilien Robespierre, one of the leaders of the French Revolution, was inspired by this saying and fought for freedom and equality.

FRIENDSHIP

'I had a friend.' So said the writer Charles Kingsley, referring to his friend-ship with F. D. Maurice, when asked about the secret of his life.

'This belonged to the best friend I ever had.' Lord Shaftesbury said this as he showed people the gold watch which had been given to him by his family housekeeper, who had taught him about Jesus.

A Persian monarch, Shah Abbis, was noted for greatly loving his people. In order to get to know his subjects better the great monarch wore differ-ent disguises so that he would not be noticed. One day Shah Abbis went to a poor man whose job was to keep the fires of the public baths burning. When lunchtime came the monarch shared the simple food which his lonely subject offered him. The Shah often visited this old man, and the old man became very fond of him. One day the Shah told the old man who he really was. The monarch expected him to ask him for some expensive gift. Instead, the old man said to him, 'You left your palace and your glory to sit with me in this dark place, to eat my coarse food, and be my friend, whether I was sad or happy. You may have bestowed priceless presents on other people, but you have given me something much more valuable: you have given me yourself. So my request now is that you never take away your gift of friendship from me.'

A judicious friend, into whose heart we may pour out our souls, and tell our corruptions as well as our comforts, is a very great privilege.
George Whitefield

A friend is a second self.
Latin proverb

A faithful friend is an image of God.
French proverb

FUNERALS
Ah, why should we wear black for the guests of God?
John Ruskin

A tramp went to David Livingstone's funeral. Afterwards he was found inconsolable, with floods of tears flowing down his cheeks. He was asked if he was a close member of the family of the heroic missionary. 'No,' replied the tramp, 'I'm not a member of his family. But we were in the same class at school, and we worked the same loom in the mill at Blantyre. We took different roads. I took the wrong road and became a drunk. David, as a young man, began to follow and serve Jesus, and that took him to Africa.'

GARDENS

Jesus was in a garden, not of delights as the first Adam, in which he destroyed himself and the whole human race, but in one of agony, in which he saved the whole human race.
Blaise Pascal

GENEROSITY

Cary Grant had starred opposite Audrey Hepburn in the film *Charade*, and afterwards he had said, 'All I want for Christmas is another movie with Audrey Hepburn.' However, when offered the part of Professor Higgins in the film *My Fair Lady*, in which Audrey Hepburn was to play Eliza Dolittle, he refused. In the London and Broadway stage show, Professor Higgins had been played by Rex Harrison, and Cary Grant said, 'Not only will I not play Higgins, if you don't put Rex Harrison in it, I won't go and see it.'
Barry Paris (quoted in The Week*)*

GENTLENESS

Be mild at their anger, humble at their boastings, to their blasphemies return your prayers, to their error your firmness in the faith; when they are cruel, be gentle; not endeavouring to imitate their ways, let us be their brethren in all kindness and moderation: but let us be followers of the Lord; for who was ever more unjustly used, more destitute, more despised?
Ignatius of Antioch

GIVING TO GOD

Just over 100 years ago a 16-year-old boy left home to seek his fortune. All his worldly possessions fitted into one bundle. Just after he had left home he came across an old neighbour, the captain of a canal boat, who asked him, 'Well, William, where are you going?'

'I don't know,' he answered. 'Father is too poor to keep me at home any longer, and says I must now make a living for myself.'

'There's no trouble about that,' said the captain. 'Be sure you start right and you'll get along fine.' William told his friend that the only trade he knew anything about was soap-making, at which he had helped his father while at home.

'Well,' said the old man, 'let me pray with you and give you a little advice, and then I will let you go.' They both knelt down on the tow-path. The dear old man prayed earnestly for William and then gave him this advice: 'Someone will soon be a leading soap-maker in New York. It can be you as well as anyone. I hope it may. Be a good man; give the Lord all that belongs to him and every dollar that you earn. Make an honest soap. Give a full pound, and I am certain that you will yet be a prosperous and rich man.'

At first William found it hard to get work. Eventually he had regular employment, became a partner and then the sole owner of the whole business. He had read in the Bible how the Jews were commanded to give one tenth of their income to the Lord. So William thought to himself: 'If the Lord will take one tenth, I will give that.' And that's what he did. For William ten cents out of every dollar was sacred, and given to the Lord's work.

He told his book-keeper to open an account for the Lord, and he made sure that one tenth of his income went into that account. As he prospered, he gave 20 per cent of his income into the Lord's account; then 30 per cent, then 40 per cent and then 50 per cent. William's surname was Colgate, and Colgate soap became famous. By the end of his life he was giving over 90 per cent of his income to 'the Lord's account'.

A farmer one day went happily, and with great joy in his heart to report to his wife and family that their best cow had given birth to twin calves, one red and one white. And he said, 'You know, I have suddenly had a feeling and impulse that we must dedicate one of these calves to the Lord. We will bring them up together, and when the time comes we will sell one and give the proceeds to the Lord's work.'

His wife asked him which calf he was going to dedicate to the Lord. 'There's no need to bother about that now,' he replied, 'we will treat them both in the same way, and when the time comes we will do as I say.'

And off he went. A few months later the farmer went into his kitchen looking very miserable. When his wife asked him what was troubling him, he answered, 'I have bad news to give you. The Lord's calf is dead.'

'But,' she said, 'you had not decided which was the Lord's calf.'

'Oh, yes,' he said, 'I had always decided that it was to be the white one, and it is the white one that has died. The Lord's calf is dead.'

We may laugh at that story, but God forbid that we should be laughing at ourselves. It is always the Lord's calf that dies. When money becomes difficult the first thing to go, with so many people, is our contribution to God's work.

Martin Lloyd-Jones

C. H. Spurgeon had just finished preaching a sermon on the subject of giving. His text had been the story of the widow who gave two mites (two very small copper coins). At the end of the service a very wealthy woman made her way haughtily towards the exit. Spurgeon watched her as she put a tiny coin into the collection box. As she passed he said to her, 'You know, the widow put in two mites!' So the woman went back and put another tiny coin into the box. But Spurgeon did not leave it at that. He then said to her, 'You know, the widow put in all she had!' Then the woman stormed angrily out of the church.

GOD

See also **Adoration of God; Atheism; Belief; Experiences of God; Giving to God; Peace; Power; Providence; Trinity; Trusting in God**

God is that, the greater than which cannot be conceived.
Anselm

Desire only God, and your heart will be satisfied.
Augustine

Dedication to God

This is the prayer of dedication to God which the father of Matthew Henry, the great Bible commentator, taught his children:

I take God the Father to be my God;
I take God the Son to be my Saviour;
I take the Holy Ghost to be my Sanctifier;
I take the Word of God to be my rule;
I take the people of God to be my people;
And I do hereby dedicate and yield my whole self to the Lord:
And I do this deliberately, freely, and forever. Amen.

The peace of God

A Japanese student named Toki Miyashina wrote this adaptation of Psalm 23 which focuses on inner peace with God:

The Lord is my Pace-setter, I shall not rush.
He makes me stop and rest for quiet intervals,
He provides me with images of stillness, which restore my serenity.
He leads me in ways of efficiency, through calmness of mind,

And His guidance is peace.
Even though I have a great many things to accomplish each day
I will not fret, for His presence is here,
His timelessness, His all-importance will keep me in balance.
He prepares refreshment and renewal in the midst of my activity
By anointing my mind with His oils of tranquillity;
My cup of joyous energy overflows.
Surely harmony and effectiveness shall be the fruits of my hours,
For I shall walk at the pace of my Lord, and dwell in His house for ever.

The presence of God

In 1896 Glasgow University conferred the degree of Doctor of Laws on David Livingstone. Afterwards he addressed a gathering of students. He bore on his body the marks of his African struggles. Severe illness on nearly 30 occasions had left him gaunt and haggard. His left arm, which had been crushed by a lion, hung limp at his side.

After describing his trials and tribulations, he said: 'Would you like me to tell you what supported me through all the years of exile among people whose language I could not understand, and whose attitude towards me was always uncertain and often hostile? It was this: "Lo, I am with you always, even unto the end of the world." On these words I staked everything, and they never failed.'

Serving God/Christ

The orphanage founder George Müller was once asked, 'What is the secret of your service?'

'There was a day when I died ...' he replied, bending over until he almost reached the floor. He continued, '... died to George Müller – his opinions, preferences, tastes and will; died to the world – its approval or censure; died to the approval or blame even of my brethren or friends; and since then I have studied only to show myself approved unto God.'

In Taiwan in 1970 the 68-year-old missionary Gladys Aylward died as she had lived – sacrificially. *The London Evening Standard* reported this event under the headline, 'The Small Woman's Last Sacrifice', as she had become ill as a result of giving away most of her bedding.

One of the orphans she had brought up on the Chinese mainland visited her just before she died, and asked her what she would like as a Christmas present. Gladys said she would love to have a cotton quilt. The orphan later discovered that when the temperature had dropped to 40 degrees below zero, Gladys had given away her quilt to an orphan and her mattress to her Chinese housemaid. Her possessions consisted of just one worn-out blanket. She caught 'flu and a few days later died of pneumonia in her sleep.

I am a little pencil in the hand of a writing God who is sending a love letter to the world.
Mother Teresa

My responsibility is always and everywhere the same: to see in my brother more even than the personality and manhood that are his. My task is always and everywhere the same: to see Christ himself.
Trevor Huddleston

In 1979 Mother Teresa was awarded the Nobel Peace Prize. As she collected her prize in Sweden she said, 'I accept the prize in the name of the poor. By serving the poor I am serving Jesus.'

The sign on the stage proclaimed, 'The Motionless Man: Make Him Laugh. Win $100.' The temptation was irresistible. For three hours boys and girls, men and women performed every antic and told every joke they could dream up. But Bill Fuqua, the Motionless Man, stood perfectly still.

Fuqua, who had an entry in *The Guinness Book of World Records* for being a champion at doing nothing, appears so motionless during his routines at shopping malls, fairgrounds and amusement parks that he's sometimes mistaken for a shop dummy.

He discovered his unique talent when he was 14 while standing in front of a Christmas tree as a joke. A woman touched him and exclaimed, 'Oh, I thought it was a real person.'

Doing nothing is really impossible – even for the Motionless Man. Fuqua attributes his feigned paralysis to hyper-elastic skin, an extremely low pulse rate and intense concentration.

The Argentinian evangelist Luis Palau says the Motionless Man reminds him of some Christians, who sit still or stand around when they should be active, speaking and on the move.

General Gordon fought for Britain during the Tai Ping Rebellion in China, and a grateful British Government wanted to reward him for his services.

But Gordon refused all money and titles. He did, however, accept a gold medal on which was inscribed his name and a record of his 39 engagements. After his death the medal could not be found. It was later discovered that he had sent it to Manchester during the famine there, and he had given his permission that it should be melted down to buy food for the starving. He wrote in his diary that day: 'The last and only thing I had in the world that I value I have given over to the Lord Jesus Christ.'

The will of God
Like anybody else, I would like to live a long life. Longevity has its place. But I am not concerned about that now. I just want to do God's will.
Martin Luther King (on the eve of his assassination)

GOSSIP
See also **Busybodies**
Gossip is vice enjoyed vicariously.
Elbert Hubbard

Those who talk about others to us will talk about us to others.
Author unknown

To guard against gossip, Augustine had a notice displayed at his dinner table. It read like this: 'Let him who takes pleasure in mauling the lives of the absent know that his own is not such as to fit him to sit at this table.' He really meant business with this notice. On one occasion, when he was entertaining some close friends, the conversation began to infringe the prohibition. Augustine burst out and said, 'Either the notice will be removed, or I, your host, will retire to my cell and leave the feast.'

The three essential rules when speaking of others are: Is it true? Is it kind? Is it necessary?
Author unknown

GRACE
In John Bunyan's *Pilgrim's Progress* the character Christian is let into Mr Interpreter's house and is shown various sights. One is a very dusty room. Mr Interpreter calls for a man to sweep the room. This causes so much dust that Christian nearly chokes. Then Interpreter tells a maid to bring some water and sprinkle the room. After that, the room is easy to sweep. Christian asks, 'What does this mean?'

Mr Interpreter tells him that the room is a picture of the heart of a person who has never embraced the Christian Gospel. The dust is his original sin and inner corruption. The man who starts to sweep is the Law. The room is only made dusty by his efforts. This shows that the Law, instead of purifying the heart from sin, revives its sense of need. The Law does not have the power to subdue sin.

The maid is a picture of the Gospel when it comes into a person's heart. Thus Bunyan illustrates how sin is overcome and the soul is made clean through faith in Christ. It is then fit for the King of glory to live in.

On his death-bed John Allen of the Salvation Army said: 'I deserve to be damned, I deserve to be in hell; but God interfered!'

John Bradford, a sixteenth-century clergyman who died as a martyr, once watched some criminals being taken off to be executed. He remarked, 'There, but for the grace of God, goes John Bradford.'

I am not what I ought to be; I am not what I wish to be; I am not what I hope to be; but by the grace of God I am what I am.
John Newton

Sir Walter Raleigh – soldier, sailor, explorer, courtier, poet, author, historian and scientist – was one of the most versatile of the great Elizabethans. It was his misfortune to outlive Queen Elizabeth. Four months after she died, in July 1603, Raleigh was imprisoned on the pretext of treason. At his trial in November he was condemned to death, and the scaffold was erected in the grounds of the Tower of London.

Raleigh denied the charge of treason to the last, and historians now acquit him of it. But in the Tower Raleigh could only look up to the 'bribeless hall' of heaven, where the King's attorney is none other than Christ himself. With this in mind, Raleigh wrote his last poem:

And when the grand twelve million jury
Of our sins, with direful fury,
Against our souls black verdicts give,
Christ pleads His death, and then we live.

Raleigh's execution was postponed until 1616. When, at last, he had to die under the axe, he met his death with unfaltering faith and courage. He had grasped Paul's teaching about grace: 'There is therefore now no condemnation for those who are in Christ Jesus.'

Dr Barnardo was walking along a dirty London street one day when a poor boy in rags asked him if he could join one of the Barnardo Homes. 'I don't know anything about you,' said the doctor. 'What have you to recommend yourself with?'

'I thought that these would be enough,' said the boy, pointing to his torn clothes.

Dr Barnardo took him up in his arms, and he joined one of the Homes that day.

GRANDMOTHERS

Brother Roger is the founder of the Taizé community, to which thousands of young people come every year from all over the world. Brother Roger writes that he was very influenced by his grandmother who, as a widow in France during the World War I, courageously welcomed refugees into her home. At the end of the war she was determined to do all she could to stop such horror reoccurring. Believing that reconciliation between Christians would help to create peace, she began by creating reconciliation within herself, and, though she came of old Protestant stock, she started going to the local Catholic Church.

Brother Roger writes: 'The two options taken by that old woman have marked my whole life. My grandmother took risks for those who were being badly treated at that time. And ... within herself she reconciled the current of faith of her Protestant background with the faith of the Catholic Church.'

GREED

See also **Money; Possessions**

A dog was crossing a river with a piece of meat in her mouth. As she spotted her own reflection in the water she thought that she saw another dog with a larger piece of meat in its mouth. She let go of her own piece of meat and attempted to snatch the other piece of meat from the other dog. This resulted in her having neither piece of meat. She could not grab the other piece of meat, as it did not exist, and the river carried her own piece of meat down stream.

Moral: This story illustrates what happens to people who always want more than they have.
One of Aesop's fables

The American actress Julia Roberts has tried to make her neighbours move elsewhere. She claims that the impoverished Castro family's shack, which backs on to her $2 million holiday home in New Mexico, spoils her view. She has offered them $30,000 to knock it down. They want $300,000.

Leonard Capsman, the writer and producer of *Dallas*, the world's most popular TV soap, died in September 1996, aged 67. *Dallas* was seen by a world audience of over 200 million, and in Britain over 27 million people watched it to see the 'Who killed J.R.?' episode. Capsman said there were four ingredients in *Dallas* which accounted for its great success: 'Greed, wealth, fame and sex.' He placed greed at the head of his list.

GROWTH

In its first year, the Coca-Cola Company managed to sell only 400 bottles of Coke.

In its first year, the Gillette Company sold only 51 razors and 168 blades.

A boy was expelled from his Latin class for slow learning. He resolved to excel in English. He was Winston Churchill.

A six-year-old boy was sent home from school with a note saying he was too stupid to learn. His name was Thomas Edison.

Louis Pasteur was reckoned to be the slowest learner in his chemistry class.

Sir Walter Scott's teacher called him a hopeless dunce.

HABITS

Julius Caesar conquered much of Western Europe for Rome. He summed up his military successes in these words: 'I came, I saw, I conquered.' This saying can be contrasted with Proverbs 16:32: 'Better is a patient man than a warrior, a man who controls his temper than one who takes a city.' It is easier to conquer a city than to conquer our own selves and tempers. If you do not shun small defects, bit by bit you will fall into greater ones.

Thomas à Kempis (The Imitation of Christ)

HEALING

See also **Dying**

Gregory of Nyssa, a fourth-century bishop, wrote the following account of the healing of his sister, Macrina:

There was with us our little girl who was suffering from an eye ailment resulting from an infectious sickness. It was a terrible and pitiful thing to see her, as the membrane around the pupil was swollen and whitened by the disease.

I went to the men's quarters where your brother Peter was Superior, and my wife went to the women's quarters to be with St Macrina. After an interval of time we were getting ready to leave but the blessed one would not let my wife go, and said she would not give up my daughter, whom she was holding in her arms, until she had given them a meal and offered them 'the wealth of philosophy'. She kissed the child as one might expect and put her lips on her eyes and, when she noticed the diseased pupil she said, 'If you do me the favour of remaining for dinner I will give you a return in keeping with this honour.' When the child's mother asked what it was, the great lady replied, 'I have some medicine which is especially effective in curing eye disease.'

We gladly remained and later started the journey home, bright and happy. Each of us told his own story on the way. My wife was telling everything in order, as if going through a treatise, and when she came to the point at which the medicine was promised, interrupting the narrative, she said, 'What have we done? How did we forget the promise, the medicine for the eyes?'

I was annoyed at our thoughtlessness, and quickly sent one of my men back to ask for the medicine, when the child, who happened to be in her nurse's arms, looked at her mother, and the mothers, fixing her gaze on the child's eyes said, 'Stop being upset by our carelessness.' She said this in a loud voice, joyfully and fearfully. 'Nothing of what was promised to us has been omitted, but the true medicine that heals disease, the cure that comes from prayer, this she has given us, and has already worked; nothing at all is left of the disease of the eyes.'

As she said this, she took our child and put her in my arms, and I also then comprehended the miracles in the gospel which I had not believed before, and I said, 'What a great thing it is for sight to be restored to the blind by the hand of God, if now his handmaiden makes much cures and has done such a thing through faith in him, a fact no less impressive than these miracles.'

Facidia is a small suburb of Rhinocorura, a city of Egypt. From this village, a woman who had been blind for ten years was brought to be blessed by Hilarion [a fourth-century hermit]. On being presented to him by the brothers (already there were many monks with him), she told him that she had bestowed all her substance on physicians. To her the saint replied: 'If what you lost on physicians you had given to the poor, Jesus the true Physician would have healed you.' Whereupon she cried aloud and implored him to have mercy on her. Then, following the example of the Saviour, he rubbed spittle on her eyes and she was immediately cured.

There would not be time if I wanted to tell you all the signs and wonders performed by Hilarion.

Jerome

The tax collector in Torgau and the counsellor in Belgern have written me to ask that I offer good advice and help for Mrs John Korner's afflicted husband. I know of no worldly help to give. If the doctors are at a loss to find a remedy, you can be sure that it is not a case of ordinary melancholy. It must, rather, be an affliction that comes from the devil, and this must be counteracted by the power of Christ with the prayer of faith. This is what we do, and what we have been accustomed to do, for a cabinet maker here was similarly afflicted with madness and we cured him by prayer in Christ's name.

Accordingly you should proceed as follows: Go to him with the deacon and two or three good men. Confident that you, as pastor of the place, are clothed with the authority of the ministerial office, lay your hands upon him and say, 'Peace be with you, dear brother, from God our Father and from our Lord Jesus Christ.' Thereupon repeat the Creed and the Lord's Prayer over him in a clear voice, and close with these words: 'O God, almighty Father, who has told us through your Son, "Truly, truly, I say to you, Whatever you ask the Father in my name, he will give it you"; who have commanded and encouraged us to pray in his name, "Ask, and you will receive", and who in like manner has said, "Call on me in the day of trouble: I will deliver you, and you will glorify me"; we unworthy sinners, relying on these your words and commands, pray for your mercy with such faith as we can muster. Graciously deign to free this man from all evil, and defeat the work that Satan has done in him, to the honour of your name and the strengthening of the faith of believers; through the same Jesus Christ, your Son, our Lord, who lives and reigns with you, world without end. Amen.'

Then, when you leave, lay your hands on the man again and say, 'These signs will follow them that believe; they shall lay hands on the sick, and they shall recover.' Do this three times, once on each of three successive days.
Martin Luther

HEAVEN
See also **Eternity**
'I saw the heavens opened, and God sitting on his great white throne.' So said Handel, explaining how he was inspired as he wrote the 'Hallelujah Chorus'.

When I get to heaven, I shall see three wonders there. The first wonder will be to see many there whom I did not expect to see; the second wonder will be to miss many people who I did expect to see; the third and greatest of all will be to find myself there.
John Newton

My idea of heaven, is eating *pates de foie gras* to the sound of trumpets.
Sydney Smith

Colonel James B. Irwin walked on the surface of the moon on 30 July 1971, and he stayed there for a record 67 hours. In later life he said, 'Jesus himself is preparing all of us who know him for a most distant journey – more distant even than the trip to the moon. The Lord wants us to be where he is throughout eternity.

HERESY
The only remedy for a false view of the cross is the cross itself.
H. B. Dehqani-Tafit (former Bishop of Jerusalem and the Middle East)

HOLINESS

A true love of God must begin with a delight in his holiness, and not with a delight in any other attribute; for no other attribute is truly lovely without this.
Jonathan Edwards

Holiness involves friendship with God. There has to be a moment in our relationship with God when he ceases to be just a Sunday acquaintance and becomes a weekday friend.
Basil Hume

I am a great enemy to flies; when I have a good book, they flock upon it and parade up and down it, and soil it. It is just the same with the devil. When our hearts are purest, he comes and soils them.
Martin Luther

HOLLYWOOD

Hollywood is a place where they'll pay you a thousand dollars for a kiss and fifty cents for your soul.
Marilyn Monroe

HOLY SPIRIT

See also **Experiences of God; Miracles**

Four steps to being filled with the Spirit
Step One: I must be filled. Say it to God in the depth of your heart. God commands it; I cannot live my life as I should live without it.

Step Two: I may be filled. Then, say as the second step: *I may be filled.* It is possible: the promise is for me. Settle that, and let all doubt vanish. These apostles, once so full of pride and of self-life, were filled with the Holy Spirit because they clave unto Jesus. And, with all your sinfulness, if you will but cling to him, you *may be filled.*

Step Three: I would be filled. Then, thirdly, say: *I would be filled.* To get the 'pearl of great price' (Matthew 13:46) you must sell all, you must give up everything. You are willing, are you not? Everything, Lord, if I may only have that. Lord, I would have it from you today.

Step Four: I shall be filled. And then comes the last step: *I shall be filled.* God longs to give it; I shall have it. Never mind whether it comes immediately, as a flood, or in deep silence; or whether it does not come today, because God is preparing you for it tomorrow. But say, *I shall be filled.* If I entrust myself to Jesus he cannot disappoint me. It is his very nature, it is his work in heaven, it is his delight to give souls the Holy Spirit in full measure. Claim it at once; *I shall.* My God, it is so solemn, it is almost awful; it is too blessed and too true – Lord, will you not do it? My trembling heart says, *I shall be filled* with the Holy Spirit. Say to God, '*Father, I shall,* for the name of my Saviour is Jesus, who saves from all sin, and who fills with the Holy Spirit. Glory to his name!'
Andrew Murray

> What God chooses, he cleanses.
> What God cleanses, he moulds.
> What God moulds, he fills.
> What God fills, he uses.

J. S. Baxter

I believe in the surprises of the Holy Spirit.
Léon Joseph (Belgian archbishop)

The evangelist John Wimber is on record as saying: 'We've had numerous occasions where God has revealed sins of people, either through a word of knowledge or a combination of that and a word of wisdom or prophecy.' He gives the following example.

He was once on an aeroplane when he turned and looked at a passenger across the aisle and saw the word 'adultery' written over his face in large letters. The letters were, of course, only perceptible to the spiritual eye. The man caught Wimber staring at him and said, 'What do you want?' Just as he was asking that, a woman's name came clearly into Wimber's mind, and he replied by enquiring of this other passenger if that name meant anything to him. The man's face paled, and he suggested they should talk in some other place.

It was a large plane with a bar, so they went to talk there. On the way the Lord spoke to Wimber again, saying, 'Tell him to turn from his adulterous affair or I am going to take him.' When they got to the bar Wimber told him that God had revealed that he was committing adultery with the woman whose name he had first mentioned and that God would take him if he did not repent. In tears, the man asked what he should do. He repented and received Christ in front of a stewardess and two other passengers at the bar. When he mentioned that the passenger in the seat beside him was his wife, Wimber suggested that the man should tell her the entire story, which he did. The man was then able to lead his wife to Christ.

HOPE

The word 'hope' I take for faith; and indeed hope is nothing else but the constancy of faith.
John Calvin

HOSPITALITY

If a man be gracious and courteous to strangers, it shows he is a citizen of the world.
Francis Bacon

Let everyone that comes be received as Christ.
St Benedict

HUMANKIND

Samuel Butler rather unflatteringly described the human body as 'A pair of pincers set over a bellows and a stewpan, and the whole thing fixed upon stilts.' The human body has 206 bones and 600 muscles. Its lungs have over three million tiny air sacs. Nearly 100,000 kilometres of arteries and capillaries transport six litres of blood around the body over 1,000 times a day. Sixty per cent of the body is fluid and 95 per cent of the body's weight consists of oxygen, nitrogen, carbon, hydrogen, phosphorus and calcium – six of the most common elements. A biologist would describe the human body as a collection of chemicals, but we may be surprised to learn that this is one of the ways in which the Bible also describes the human body. 'The Lord formed man from the dust of the earth' (Genesis 2:7), and when we die 'the dust returns to the ground it came from' (Ecclesiastes 12:7).

HUMILITY

It appears from Luke's Gospel that Jesus was born in the outhouse of an inn. There is, however, a tradition dating from the second century that Jesus was born in a cave. In the fourth century the Emperor Constantine the Great had a church built over this cave. Later a much more beautiful building was erected there. The Church of the Nativity which today stands over the cave is similar to the one built there over 1,600 years ago.

Although the church is full of gaudy jewels and some rather unlovely statues, it is nevertheless a monument to the birth of Jesus Christ. Kings and princes used to ride in on their horses through the large entrance. However, today a horse and rider could never get in. The door is so low that one has to stoop down in order to enter.

This is often used as an illustration of how people can only come to Jesus Christ if they are prepared to bow before him.

Jesus' life began in a borrowed stable and ended in a borrowed tomb.
Alfred Plummer

Once St Francis came in from the wood where he prayed. Brother Masseo met him and tried to find out just how humble Francis was.

'Why you?' asked Brother Masseo. 'The whole world goes after you. But you are not a handsome man, you have no great knowledge or wisdom, you are not noble. Why you?'

Francis stood still for a long time and then said, 'To do the wondrous work God had in mind to do, he chose me. For God has chosen the foolish things of the world to confound the wise; the mean, contemptible, feeble things of the world to confound the noble and great; so that the grandeur of goodness should proceed from God, and not from his creature; so that no flesh should boast, but that God alone should be honoured.'
The Little Flowers of St Francis

When a certain rhetorician was asked what was the chief rule of eloquence he replied, 'Delivery.' What was the second rule? 'Delivery.' What was the third rule? 'Delivery.' So if you ask me about the precepts of the Christian religion, first, second, third and always I would answer, 'Humility.'
Augustine

We may as well try to see without eyes, or live without breath, as to live in the spirit of religion without humility.
William Law

Humility is to make the right estimate of one's self.
C. H. Spurgeon

We must view humility as one of the most essential things that character-
ize true Christianity.
Jonathan Edwards

The foundation of our philosophy is humility.
John Chrysostom

HUSBANDS

See also **Marriage**
Being a husband is a whole-time job. That is why so many husbands fail.
They cannot give their entire attention to it.
Arnold Bennett

HYPOCRISY

The Interpreter took Mercy and Christiana into the garden to a tree
whose inside was all rotten and gone, and yet it grew and had leaves. Then
Mercy said, 'What is the meaning of this?'

'This tree,' said Interpreter, 'whose outside is fair, and whose inside is
rotten, is what many may be compared to who are in God's garden. With
their mouths, they speak high about God, but indeed will do nothing for
him; whose leaves are fair, but their heart is good for nothing but to be
tinder for the devil's tinder-box.'

Then, as Interpreter, Mercy and Christiana went outside, they saw a
little robin with a great spider in his mouth. So the Interpreter said, 'Look
there.' So they looked, and Mercy wondered. But Christiana said, 'What
a disparagement it is to such a pretty little bird as the robin redbreast. He
is also a bird above many, that loves to maintain a kind of sociableness
with man. I thought they lived on the crumbs of bread, or upon other
such harmless matter. I like him worse than I did.'

The Interpreter replied, 'This robin is a very suitable image of some
who profess to believe; for to look at they are like this robin, with a pretty
song, colour, and bearing; they seem also to have a very great love for
those who make a sincere profession; and above all, to desire to associate
with and to be in their company, as if they could live upon the good
man's crumbs. They pretend also, that that is why they frequent the
house of the godly, and the appointments of the Lord; but when they are

by themselves, like the robin, they can catch and gobble up spiders, they can change their diet, drink iniquity, and swallow down sin like water.'
John Bunyan (Pilgrim's Progress)

I

ILLNESS
See also **Suffering**
Paul McCartney was knighted in 1997. At the time he said about his wife Linda, who had been battling against breast cancer, 'Linda has not been well the past year or so, although she is doing very well now. It's very difficult when you get that kind of situation in your life.'

IMPRISONMENT
See also **Suffering; Torture**
John Bunyan was imprisoned for preaching the Gospel. In his cell he wrote:

The parting with my wife and poor children hath often been to me in this place, as the pulling of the flesh from my bones; and that not only because I am somewhat fond of these great mercies, but also because I should have often brought to my mind the many hardships, miseries, and wants that my poor family was like to meet with, should I be taken from them, especially my poor blind child, who lay nearer my heart than all I had besides. O the thought of the hardship I thought my blind one might go under, would break up my heart to pieces.

But yet, recalling myself, thought I, I must venture all with God, though it goeth to the quick to leave you; O I saw in this condition, I was a man who was pulling down his house upon the head of his wife and children; yet thought I, I must do it, I must do it.

INCARNATION
See also **Jesus Christ**
The central miracle asserted by Christians is the incarnation. They say that God became man.
C. S. Lewis

INDECISION
We know what happens to people who stay in the middle of the road. They get run over.
Aneurin Bevan

INDIFFERENCE

'Hear no evil, see no evil, speak no evil.' This saying is traced back to a legend about the Three Wise Monkeys which were carved over the door of the Sacred Stable at Nikko in Japan in the seventeenth century. One monkey has its hands over its ears, the second monkey has its hands covering its eyes and the third monkey's hands are covering its mouth.

The traditional Yorkshireman's motto is:
Here all, see all, say nowt;
Aight all, sup all, pay nowt;
And if ever tha does owt for nowt,
Do it for thisen.

INEQUALITY

See also **Equality**

All animals are equal but some are more equal than others.
George Orwell (Animal Farm)

INFALLIBILITY

I'm sorry we're late, we misread the timetables. But there – nobody's infallible.
Geoffrey Fisher, Archbishop of Canterbury, to Pope John XXIII

JESUS CHRIST

See also **Bible:** Christ in the Bible; **Cross of Jesus; Humility; Incarnation**

To put the matter at its simplest, Jesus Christ came to make bad men good.

James Denney

Latimer! Latimer! Latimer! Be careful what you say. Henry the king is here. *(Pause.)* Latimer! Latimer! Latimer! Be careful what you say. The King of kings is here.

Hugh Latimer (preaching before Henry VIII)

Christ is not valued at all, unless he is valued above all.

Augustine

Christ's character was more wonderful than the greatest miracle.

Alfred, Lord Tennyson

Apart from Christ we know neither what our life nor our death is; we do not know what God is nor what we ourselves are.

Blaise Pascal

Jesus' historicity

Nero punished with the utmost refinement of cruelty, a class hated for their abominations, who were commonly called Christians. Chrestus, from whom their name derived, was executed at the hands of the Procurator Pontius Pilate in the reign of Tiberius.

Tacitus

At that time lived Jesus, a wise man, if he may be called a man, for he performed many wonderful works. He was a teacher of such men as received the truth with pleasure. He drew over to him many Jews and Gentiles. This was the Christ; and when Pilate, at the instigation of the chief men among us, had condemned him to the cross, they who before had

conceived an affection for him, did not cease to adhere to him; for, on the third day, he appeared to them alive again, the divine prophets having foretold these and many wonderful things concerning him. And the sect of the Christians, so called from him, subsists to this time.
Josephus

Jesus' person
Jesus is either God, or he is not good.
Anselm

Pythagoras, Epicurus, Socrates, Plato, these are the torches of the world; Christ is the light of day.
Victor Hugo

In his life Christ is an example,
showing us how to live;
In his death he is a sacrifice,
satisfying for our sins;
In his resurrection, a conqueror;
In his ascension, a king;
In his intercession, a high priest.
Martin Luther

Brethren, we ought so to think of Jesus Christ as of God.
2 Clement *(Early Church sermon)*

Take hold of Jesus as a man and you will discover that he is God.
Martin Luther

They replied, 'You are the eschatological manifestation of the ground of our being, the kerygma of which we find the ultimate meaning in our inter-personal relationships.'
Author unknown

This man was, and is, the Son of God, or else a madman or something worse.
C. S. Lewis

He ate, drank, slept, walked, was weary, sorrowful, rejoicing, he wept and laughed; he knew hunger and thirst and sweat; he talked, he toiled, he prayed … so that there was no difference between him and other men, save only this, that he was God and had no sin.
Martin Luther

Christ either deceived mankind by conscious fraud, or he was himself deluded, or he was divine. There is no getting out of this trilemma.
George Duncan

He became what we are that he might make us what he is.
Athanasius of Alexandria

Jesus praying for us
If I could hear Christ praying for me in the next room, I would not fear a million enemies. Yet distance makes no difference. He *is* praying for me.
Robert Murray M'Cheyne

Jesus our righteousness
Methought I saw, with the eyes of my soul, Jesus Christ at God's right hand; there I say, was my righteousness; so that wherever I was, or whatever I was doing, God could not say of me, he wants my righteousness, for that was just before him. I saw also, moreover, that it was not my good frame of heart that made my righteousness better, nor yet my bad frame of that which made my righteousness worse; for my righteousness was Jesus Christ himself, 'the same yesterday, and today and for ever.' Now did the chains fall off my legs indeed.
John Bunyan (Grace Abounding)

Jesus our sacrifice
Pepita was a poor gipsy girl. One day the famous Dusseldorf artist, Stenburg, saw her and realized that she would make a beautiful model. On her first visit to his studio she was amazed by the sight of his many paintings. Her eye was caught by an unfinished picture of the crucifixion, which Stenburg had been commissioned to paint by the wealthy church of St Jerome.

'Who is that?' asked the girl, pointing to the most prominent figure.
'The Christ,' answered Stenburg carelessly.
'What is being done to him?' she asked.

'He is being crucified,' the artist replied impatiently.

'Who are those people around him – those with the bad faces?' asked Pepita.

'Now, look here,' said the painter. 'I can't talk to you! You must stand still and not ask questions.'

The girl didn't dare to speak again, but she gazed and wondered. She was fascinated by the picture of the Christ and was unable to get it out of her thoughts. Then one day she ventured to ask: 'Why did they crucify him? Was he bad – very bad?'

'No, very good,' replied Stenburg.

That answer made Pepita even more curious, but she did not pluck up courage to ask her next question until the following day: 'If he was so good, why did they crucify him?'

The eager, questioning face moved the artist. 'Listen. I will tell you once and for all, and then you must ask no more questions.' He proceeded to tell her the story of Jesus' crucifixion. This was new to Pepita, but so old to the artist that it had ceased to touch him. He could paint that dying agony without being moved, but the thought of it deeply moved Pepita's heart. She sighed and reverently gazed on the bleeding, agonizing picture of the suffering Christ.

When Pepita came to the studio for the last time, she said: 'Signor, you must love him very much, do you not, when he has done all that for you?' Stenburg's face flushed crimson. He was ashamed and turned away. Her plaintive words, however, continued to ring in his heart, disturbing and distressing him day and night.

Some months later a large crowd trooped into the house of a poor person near the city walls. When Stenburg asked who they were, he was told, 'A pack of interfering reformers.' His curiosity got the better of him, and he went into the house. This resulted in his conversion to Christ. He found what he had longed for – a living faith. He now longed to share this good news about redemption through Christ's death and to tell everyone about Jesus' wonderful love. 'But,' he said to himself, 'I cannot speak. If I tried, I could never articulate what I want to say. It burns in my heart, but I cannot express it… But I *can* paint!' He fell to his knees and asked God to help him to paint in a worthy way. His prayer was answered, and he produced a painting of the crucifixion that touched the hearts and lives of many people.

He would not sell it, but he presented it to his own city of Dusseldorf, to be displayed in the public gallery. There the people of Dusseldorf and visitors from all over the world flocked to see it. Voices were hushed and hearts melted as they stood before it and pondered the words written so distinctly beneath it:

All this I did for thee;
What hast thou done for Me?

Stenburg himself used to go there, watching from an obscure corner of the gallery, as the people came to look at his picture. He prayed that God would bless the painted sermon. One day he noticed a poor girl weeping bitterly in front of it. He went to her. It was Pepita, his gipsy model. 'Oh, Signor, if only he had loved me so!' she said. 'I am only a poor gipsy. For you there is love, but not for such as I.' And she burst into tears again.

'Pepita, it was also for you,' explained the artist. He was now only too eager to answer all her questions. He told her about the wonderful life, sacrificial death and amazing resurrection of Jesus. Pepita listened and believed, and she received the Lord Jesus Christ into her heart, there and then.

Two years later, while Stenburg was comfortably seated in his home beside blazing pine logs on a bitterly cold night, his servant showed in a man who had asked to see him urgently. Stenburg followed this stranger through the night to a clearing in the forest where there was a gipsy encampment. There, in a tent lit by the light of the moon, he found Pepita. Her face was pinched and hollow. She was dying. At the sound of the artist's voice she opened her eyes and said, 'He has come for me! He holds out his hands! They are bleeding! And he says: "For thee. All for you. All this I did for you." ' She lay still for a moment, and then she died.

Many years after Stenburg's death a young nobleman drove into Dusseldorf in his splendid carriage. While his horses were being watered and fed at an inn, he wandered into the famous picture gallery. He was rich, young and intelligent, and the world lay at his feet, with all its treasures within his grasp. But he stood in front of Stenburg's picture, transfixed. He read and re-read the words beneath it. He could not tear himself away. The love of Christ gripped his soul. Hours passed by, the light faded and the curator had to touch the weeping nobleman's shoulder and tell him that the gallery was closing. Night had come, but for this young man it was dawn. He was Count Zinzendorf. He returned to the inn and went back to Paris in his carriage. From that moment he threw his life, fortune and fame at the feet of the One who had spoken to his heart in that gallery.

Stenburg's picture is no longer in the gallery at Dusseldorf, as both gallery and picture were destroyed in a fire. But the picture had preached, and God had used it to speak about his Son, Jesus Christ.

Jesus' second coming

I do not think that in the last forty years I have lived one conscious hour that was not influenced by the thought of our Lord's return.
Lord Shaftesbury

As Dr Horatius Bonar drew his curtains each night he repeated to himself the words, 'Perhaps tonight, Lord!' As he woke, he drew back the curtains, looked into the sky, and said, 'Perhaps today, Lord!' He expected the Lord to return at any moment.

Jesus our sin-bearer
He [Christ, our Sin-bearer] is not like Moses who only shows sin, but rather like Aaron who bears sin.
Martin Luther

Jesus became the greatest liar, perjurer, thief, adulterer and murderer than mankind has ever known – not because he committed these sins but because he was actually made sin for us.
Martin Luther

Jesus the way to God
Beyond that which is found in Jesus Christ, the human race has not and never will progress.
Coleridge

Jesus does not give recipes that show the way to God as other teachers of religion do. He is himself the way.
Karl Barth

Jews and Christians
Jews have God's promise and if we Christians have it, too, then it is only as those chosen with them, as guests in their house, that we are new wood grafted onto their tree.
Karl Barth

Job, book of
The greatest poem of ancient and modern times.
Alfred, Lord Tennyson

KINDNESS

Kindness is a language the blind can see and the deaf can hear.
Author unknown

In her mid-teens April Fleming, an American schoolgirl, was dying of a blood disorder called poly-cythemia vera. In 1994 an American organization called Make-a-Wish Foundation asked April to make a wish which they would grant for her. To their surprise, instead of asking for a treat for herself, April asked the Foundation to buy Christmas presents for homeless children. All over America, people heard about April's wish, and sent gifts and donations to her, which she used to make gift parcels for homeless people in Olympia, Washington. She died at the age of 17. Her wish was that 'everyone practice a random act of kindness to help a fellow human being who is in need.'

KINGDOM OF GOD

The gospel of Jesus is *autobasilea*, the kingdom himself.
Origen

If you want to work for the kingdom of God, and to enter into it, there is just one condition to be first accepted. You must enter it as children, or not at all.
John Wesley

There can be no kingdom of God in the world without the kingdom of God in our hearts.
Albert Schweitzer

KNOWLEDGE

He that knows not and knows not that he knows not is a fool: shun him.
He that knows not and knows that he knows not is a child: teach him.
He that knows and knows not that he knows is asleep: wake him.
He that knows and knows that he knows is a wise man: follow him.
Arabic proverb

LORD'S SUPPER

The sacrament is the eaten word of God.
Martin Luther

In his *Marrow of Ecclesiastical History* the seventeenth-century writer Samuel Clarke reports that when asked what she believed about the presence of Christ in the sacrament, Queen Elizabeth I replied:

> 'Twas God the word that spake it,
> He took the bread and brake it;
> And what the word did make it,
> That I believe, and take it.

The four views which have unhappily divided the Christian world on the subject of the sacrament [i.e. Holy Communion, the Lord's Supper or the Mass] are the following:

1. The Romish doctrine, or transubstantiation. This maintains the absolute change of the elements into the actual body and blood of Christ; so that though the elements of bread and wine remain present to the senses, they are no longer what they seem, being changed into the body, blood, and divinity of Christ.
2. The Lutheran view, called consubstantiation. This maintains that after consecration the body and blood of Christ are substantially present, but nevertheless that the bread and wine are present, unchanged.
3. The Anglican view – that Christ is present in the sacrament only after the spiritual manner, and that his body and blood are eaten by the faithful after a spiritual, and not after a carnal manner, to the maintenance of their spiritual life and their growth in grace.
4. The Zwinglian view, which declares the sacrament to be no channel of grace, but only a commemorative feast, admitting only a figurative presence of Christ's body and blood.

Alas! that prisons should have been peopled, and thousands immolated on the pyre, for the sake of opinions; and that nothing but death could

atone for the horrible crime of individual judgment, instead of allowing each to stand or fall to their own master.
John Foxe (The Book of Martyrs)

LOVE

> To my God a heart of flame;
> To my fellow man a heart of love;
> To myself a heart of steel.

Augustine

He does much who loves much.
Thomas à Kempis

When William Penn founded a new city as a home of refuge for persecuted people he called it 'Philadelphia'. And that is what every church is meant to be – a haven of brotherly and sisterly love.

Charity [love] means nothing else than to love God for himself above all creatures, and to love one's fellow men for God's sake as one loves oneself.
The Cloud of Unknowing *(author unknown)*

Beware you are not swallowed up in books! An ounce of love is worth a pound of knowledge.
John Wesley

It is our care for the helpless, our practice of loving kindness, that brands us in the eyes of many of our opponents. 'Look!' they say. 'How they love one another! Look how they are prepared to die for one another.'
Tertullian

MARRIAGE

See also **Husbands**

Punch's most famous joke was published in January 1845: 'Advice to people intending to marry: Don't.'

MARTYRDOM

See also **Discipleship**; **Mission:** Jim Elliot; **Persecution**; **Prophetic messages**; **Suffering**

The history of Christian martyrdom is, in fact, the history of Christianity itself; for it is in the arena, at the stake, and in the dungeon that the religion of Christ has won its most glorious triumphs.

William Bramley-Moore's Introduction to Foxe's Book of Martyrs

Blind Chang (Chinese Christian)

Chang Men was one of the many thousands of Chinese Christians who died during the Boxer uprising of 1900. Chang became blind in his thirties, and his character was then accurately summed up by his nickname. 'Wu so pu wei te', meaning 'One without a particle of good in him'. His neighbours believed that he had been struck blind as a judgement on his evil way of life. He threw his wife and daughter out of his home, gambled, stole and became a womanizer.

When Chang learned that blind people were being cured at a mission hospital he went there. As a result he received both physical and spiritual sight. He longed to be baptized as a Christian, and was told that if he went home and told his village about Jesus Christ, a missionary would visit him and then baptize him. When James Webster visited Chang five months later he discovered that God had been greatly blessing Chang as a faithful evangelist. Webster was inundated with over 400 people wanting to become Christians.

Later Chang lost his eyesight again, after a Chinese doctor operated on him, trying to improve his partial sight. However, this did not deter Chang, who became well known as an itinerant blind Christian evangelist, able to quote nearly all of the New Testament by heart, as well as many complete chapters from the Old Testament.

The Boxer rebels came across blind Chang in Tsengkow in Manchuria. They captured 50 Christians there but were told that for every one they killed a further 10 would appear, and that they needed to deal with the ring leader of the Christians, blind Chang. The Boxers said they would free their 50 Christian prisoners if one of them would tell them where blind Chang was. No one betrayed Chang, but one of the 50 managed to escape and went and told Chang what was happening.

Chang went to the Boxers at once. But he refused to worship the god of war in the temple. He was put on an open cart and paraded through the town to a cemetery. As he went through the crowds Chang sang a song he had learned in the Christian hospital:

Jesus loves me, He who died
Heaven's gate to open wide;
He will wash away my sin,
Let His little child come in.
Jesus loves me, He will stay,
Close beside me all the way;
If I love Him when I die,
He will take me home on high.

The last words blind Chang uttered before the Boxers decapitated him were 'Heavenly Father, receive my spirit.'

John Huss (fifteenth-century Bohemian preacher)

John Huss was a Bohemian by birth, and born in the village of Hussinetz, in about 1380. His parents gave him the best education they could bestow, and, having acquired a tolerable knowledge of the classics at a private school, he was then sent to Prague University, where he soon became conspicuous by his talents and industry...

As pastor of the church of Bethlehem in Prague, and rector of the university, Huss soon became famous for his preaching and bold proclamation of the truth which quickly attracted the notice and excited the malignity of the Pope and his followers.

The principal reason which aroused Huss's indignation was a bull published by Pope John XXIII which promised remission of sins to everyone who joined his forces against Ladislaus, King of Naples. When the bull was published in Prague, Huss did not refrain from preaching against it as repugnant to the spirit of the Christian faith. The Pope summoned Huss to Rome, and, upon his refusing to comply, excommunicated him, and forbade divine service to be performed in all the churches in Prague, except for one, so long as Huss remained in the city. To avoid disturbances, Huss moved to Hussinetz.

The teachings of the English reformer, Wycliffe, were eagerly received in Bohemia by many people, especially by John Huss and his friend and fellow-martyr, Jerome of Prague.

The Pope summoned Huss to appear before the court at Rome to answer the accusations levelled against him about his preaching. Eventually three proctors appeared for Dr Huss before Cardinal Colonna: they pleaded an excuse for Huss's absence, and said they were ready to answer on his behalf. But the cardinal declared him contumacious, and, accordingly, excommunicated him. Notwithstanding such a severe decree, and an expulsion from his church in Prague, he moved again to Hussinetz, where he continued to promulgate the truth, both from the pulpit and with the pen.

In November 1414 a general council assembled at Constance in Germany to resolve the dispute between three people contesting for the papal throne: John, supported by the Italians; Gregory, supported by the French, and Benedict supported by the Spaniards. John Huss was summoned to appear before this council together with a certificate of safe conduct which said, 'You shall let John Huss pass, stop, stay, and return freely, without any hindrance whatever.' Notwithstanding the promise of the emperor to give him safe conduct to and from Constance, no attention was paid to the imperial pledge; but, according to the maxim of this same council, that 'faith is not to be kept with heretics,' when Huss entered the city he was arrested, and imprisoned in the palace.

While Huss was in prison the council acted like the inquisitors. They condemned all the teaching of Wycliffe and ordered his remains to be exhumed, and burned to ashes, which was carried out.

When Huss was brought before the council he was accused of twenty-six heresies. The council pronounced him a heretic condemning him to be burned as such, unless he recanted. Huss was then thrown into a filthy prison, where, during the day, he was so laded with chains that he could hardly move, and at night was fastened by his hands to a ring on the prison wall.

Soon after Huss had been condemned four bishops and two lords were sent by the emperor to the prison, in order to prevail on Huss to recant. But Huss called God to witness, with tears in his eyes, that he was not conscious of having preached or written anything against God's truth, or against the faith of his orthodox church. The deputies then represented the great wisdom and authority of the council: to which Huss replied, 'Let them send the meanest person of that council, who can convince me by argument from the word of God, and I will submit my judgement to him.' The deputies, finding they could not make any impression on him, departed, greatly astonished at the strength of his resolve.

On 4th July Huss, for the last time, was brought before the council. After a long examination he was commanded to abjure, which, without hesitation, he refused to do. The Bishop of Lodi then preached a sermon concerning the destruction of heretics, from the text, 'Let the body of sin be destroyed.' The council then censured him for being obstinate and incorrigible, and ordained that he should be degraded from the priesthood, his books publicly burnt, and himself delivered to the secular powers.

Huss received the sentence without the slightest emotion; and then knelt down, lifted up his eyes towards heaven, exclaiming, with the magnanimity of a primitive martyr, 'May thy infinite mercy, O my God! pardon this injustice of mine enemies. Thou knowest the injustice of my accusations: how deformed with crimes I have been represented; how I have been oppressed with worthless witnesses, and a false condemnation; yet, O my God! let that mercy of thine, which no tongue can express, prevail with thee not to avenge my wrongs.'

But these excellent sentences were received as so many expressions of treason, and only tended to inflame his adversaries. Accordingly, the bishops appointed by the council stripped him of his priestly garments, degraded him, and put a paper mitre on his head, on which they painted three devils, with this inscription: 'Heresiarch' [Heretic]. This mockery was received by the martyr with an air of unconcern, and seemed to give him dignity rather than disgrace. A serenity appeared in his looks, which indicated that his soul was approaching the realms of everlasting happiness...

After the ceremony of degradation the bishops delivered him to the emperor, who handed him over to the Duke of Bavaria. His books were burnt at the gates of the church; and on July 6th he was led to the suburbs of Constance to be burnt alive.

Having reached the place of execution, he fell on his knees, sung several portions from the Psalms, and looked steadfastly towards heaven, saying, 'Into thy hands, O Lord! do I commit my spirit: thou hast redeemed me, O most good and faithful God.'

As soon as the chain was put around him at the stake, he said, with a smiling countenance, 'My Lord Jesus Christ was bound with a harder chain than this for my sake: why, then, should I be ashamed of this old rusty one?' Then he prayed: 'Lord Jesus Christ, it is for the sake of the gospel and the preaching of the word that I patiently undergo this ignominious death.'

When the faggots were piled around him, the Duke of Bavaria was officious as to desire him to abjure. 'No,' he said, 'I never preached any doctrine of an evil tendency; and what I taught with my lips I now seal with my blood.' He then said to the executioner, 'You are now going to burn a goose (the meaning of Huss's name in Bohemian), but in a century you will have a swan whom you can neither roast nor boil.' If this were spoken in prophecy, he must have alluded to Martin Luther, who came about a hundred years after him, and had a swan for his arms.

As soon as the faggots were lighted, the martyr sang a hymn, with so cheerful a voice, that he was heard above the cracklings of the fire and the noise of the multitude. At length his voice was interrupted by the flames, which soon put an end to his existence. His ashes were collected, and, by order of the council, thrown into the Rhine, lest his adherents should honour them as relics.

John Foxe (The Book of Martyrs)

Polycarp (bishop in the Early Church)

Polycarp, bishop of Smyrna, was the leading Christian figure in the Roman province of Asia in the reign of the Emperor Antoninus Pius. According to Irenaeus, Polycarp 'had fellowship with John [the apostle] and with the others who had seen the Lord'. Polycarp's long life made him a very important link between the apostles and the Early Church. E. C. E. Owen gives this account of Polycarp's martyrdom:

Late in the day Polycarp's pursuers came up together and found him hiding in a cottage, lying in an upper room. It was within Polycarp's power to flee from there to another place, but he refused to do so, saying, 'God's will be done.'

So when Polycarp heard them arrive he came down and talked with them. The soldiers were amazed at his age and his courage and that so much trouble had been taken to arrest such an elderly man.

The soldiers brought Polycarp back into the city, riding on a donkey. The head of the police, Herod, met him. Herod's father, Nicetes, transferred Polycarp into a carriage, sat next to him, and tried to make him change his mind. Nicetes urged Polycarp, 'Tell me, what harm is done if one says that Caesar is Lord. Go on, make a sacrifice to Caesar, and then you will save your skin.'

To start with Polycarp made no reply, but as they pressed him, he said, 'I do not intend to do what you advise me.'

Once they had failed to persuade Polycarp they dragged him from the carriage into the stadium... The Proconsul was insistent and repeated, 'Swear, and we will release you; deny Christ.'

Polycarp replied: 'Eighty and six years have I served him, and he has done me no wrong; how then can I blaspheme my King who saved me?'

Still the Proconsul urged Polycarp: 'Swear by the genius of Caesar.'

'If you really think that I would, "Swear by the genius of Caesar" then you forget who I am. Take note, I am a Christian. If you want to learn the Christian faith, appoint a day, and grant me a hearing.'

The Proconsul replied, 'I have wild beasts and if you do not change your mind I will throw you to them.'

Polycarp said, 'Order them to be brought. We are not allowed to change our minds from what is good to what is evil, only to change from what is evil to what is good.'

The Proconsul said, 'As you despise the wild beasts, you will be destroyed by fire, if you do not change your mind.'

So Polycarp said, 'The fire you threaten me with only burns for a short time and then it goes out. You are ignorant of the future fire of judgment which is never put out and which is reserved for the ungodly. So what are you waiting for? Do what you want to do. I have to be burnt alive.'

This was no sooner said than done. In a moment the mob collected logs and faggots from the workshops and the baths and the Jews proved to be especially zealous about this, as usual. When the pyre had been completed they were about to nail Polycarp to the stake, but he said, 'Let me be as I am: He that gave me power to abide the fire will grant me too, without your making me fast with nails, to abide untroubled on the pyre.'

So they did not nail him to the stake but just bound him to it. Polycarp put his hands behind him and was bound, like a godly ram out of a great flock for an offering, a whole burnt offering made ready and acceptable to God. Then he looked up to heaven and prayed:

'O Lord God Almighty, you are the Father of your much loved and blessed Son Jesus Christ, through whom we have received our knowledge of you. You are the God of the angels and the powers and the God of the whole creation and of everyone who worships you. I praise you that you have counted me worthy of this day and hour so that I can be counted as one of the martyrs in the suffering of Christ and then to the resurrection to eternal life of both the body and the soul with the Holy Spirit. May I be welcomed with them today into your presence as an acceptable sacrifice. As you planned that this should happen, may it now be fulfilled since you are the faithful and true God. On account of this and for every other reason I praise you, bless you, and glorify you through the everlasting and heavenly high priest Jesus Christ, your much loved Son. It is through him we come to you in the company of the Holy Spirit, to whom we give glory now and for ever. Amen.'

As soon as Polycarp had completed his prayer and offered up his Amen the fire was kindled.

Ridley and Latimer (sixteenth-century Reformers)
On the 17th October, 1555, those two pillars of Christ's church, Dr Nicholas Ridley, Bishop of London, and Mr Hugh Latimer, sometime Bishop of Worcester, were burnt in one fire at Oxford – men ever memorable for their piety, learning, and incomparable ornaments and gifts of grace, joined with no less commendable sincerity of life.

Dr Ridley, born in Northumberland, entered the Cambridge University, where, in a short time, he became famed for his singular aptness, and was called to higher offices in the university, and was then made head of Pembroke Hall, and there made doctor of divinity. Then he went to Paris, and on his return was made chaplain to King Henry VIII, and later promoted to the bishopric of Rochester, and from there, in King Edward's days, translated to that of London.

Dr Ridley was first brought to a knowledge of Christ and his gospel by reading Bertram's book on the sacrament; and his conference with Archbishop Cranmer, and with Peter Martyr, did much to confirm him in that belief. Being now, by the grace of God, thoroughly converted to the true way, he was as constant and faithful in the right knowledge which the Lord had revealed unto him, as he was before blind and zealous in his old ignorance, and so long as the power and authority of the state defended the gospel, and supported the happiness of the church, his influence was mighty for spiritual good. But after it pleased God (in his wise providence) to bereave us of our stay, it taking from us King Edward, the whole state of the Church of England was left desolate and open to the enemy's hand: so that Bishop Ridley, after the accession of Queen Mary, was one of the first upon whom they laid their hands, and sent to prison: first in the Tower, and from there conveyed, with the Archbishop of Canterbury [Cranmer] and Mr Latimer, to Oxford, and with them confined in the common prison of Bocardo...

At the age of fourteen [Latimer] was sent to Cambridge University. Latimer, like St Paul, was both zealous and misguided. He confesses that as a priest he was so servile an observer of the Romish decrees, that in the celebration of mass his conscience was much troubled lest he had insufficiently mingled his wine with water; and, moreover, he believed that he should never be damned if he became a professed friar, with many other like superstitions.

Mr Thomas Bilney, perceiving that Latimer had a great zeal, although, like that of some of the Judaising teachers, not according to knowledge, felt a brotherly pity towards him, and began to consider by what means he might expound to this ignorant brother the way of God more perfectly, even as Aquila and Priscilla did to Apollos. Impressed with these feelings, after a short time he came to Mr Latimer's study, and asked him to hear his own confession; the result of which interview was, that Latimer's understanding was so enlightened by God's good Spirit, that immediately he forsook the study of the school doctors, and other such philosophers falsely so called, and became an earnest student of the Bible, and of that divinity which centres in the cross of Christ. He was a changed character, for he hated that which he had loved, and he now loved that which he had hated. Jesus, the Son of God, had been revealed to him, and, like the apostle, in faith and obedience he was now ready to ask, 'Lord, what wilt thou have me to do?'

After Latimer preached he gave the people certain cards out of the 5th, 6th, and 7th chapters of St Matthew, in the study of which they might, not only then, but at all other times, occupy their time... he quite overthrew all hypocritical and external ceremonies, not tending to the furtherance of God's holy Word and sacraments... he wished the Scriptures to be in English, in order that the common people might be enabled to learn their duty to God and to their neighbours.

To relate the noise and alarm the preaching of these sermons occasioned at Cambridge would require too much time and space. First came out the prior of Black Friars, named Buckenham, who attempted to prove that it was not expedient for the Scriptures to be in English, lest the ignorant and vulgar sort might be running into some inconvenience...

Mr Latimer, being thus persecuted by the friars, doctors, and masters of that university, about the year 1529, continued, notwithstanding the malice of these adversaries, preaching in Cambridge for about three years...

Mr Latimer was, at length, cited before the cardinal for heresy. He was brought to London, where he was greatly molested, and detained a long time from his cure, being summoned thrice every week before the said bishops, to vindicate his preaching, and to subscribe to certain articles or propositions, devised by the instigation of his enemies...

Mr Latimer continued in his laborious episcopal functions until the passing of the Six Articles. Being then much distressed through the straitness of the times, he felt that he must either sacrifice a good conscience or else forsake his bishopric; accordingly he did the latter. When he visited London, he was imprisoned in the Tower, where he remained until King Edward came to the crown, when the golden mouth of this English Chrysostom was opened again. He often affirmed that the preaching of the Gospel would cost him his life, for which he was cheerfully prepared; for after the death of King Edward, and not long after Mary had been proclaimed queen, Mr Latimer was arrested and brought to London.

When Mr Latimer entered Smithfield, he merrily said that Smithfield had long groaned for him. He was then brought before the council, where he patiently bore all the mocks and taunts of the scornful Papists, and was again sent to the Tower.

After the appearing of Dr Cranmer, Archbishop of Canterbury, before the Pope's delegate and the Queen's Commissioners in St Mary's Church at Oxford, about the 12th of September [1555], on the 28th of the said month another commission was sent down to Oxford from Cardinal Pole, to John White, Bishop of Lincoln, Dr Brooks, Bishop of Gloucester, and Dr Holyman, Bishop of Bristol, saying that they should examine and judge Mr Latimer and Dr Ridley, for sundry erroneous opinions that Hugh Latimer and Nicholas Ridley did maintain in open disputations held in Oxford, in the months of May, June, and July, in the year 1554...

The Articles which condemned Ridley and Latimer
In the name of God, Amen. We, John of Lincoln, James of Gloucester, and John of Bristol, bishops, etc.

1. We do object to thee, Nicholas Ridley, and to thee, Hugh Latimer, jointly and severally, first, that thou, Nicholas Ridley, in this high University of Oxford, in the year 1554, hast affirmed, and openly defended and maintained, and in many other times and places besides, that the true and natural body of Christ, after the consecration of the priest, is not really present in the sacrament of the altar.
2. That thou hast publicly affirmed and defended that in the sacrament of the altar remaineth still the substance of bread and wine.
3. That thou hast openly affirmed, and obstinately maintained, that in the mass is no propitiatory sacrifice for the living and the dead.

[Ridley was the first to be examined by the three Commissioners.] After examination upon the above articles, the Bishop of Lincoln concluded: 'Mr Ridley, I am sorry to see such stubbornness in you, that by no means you will be persuaded to acknowledge your errors, and receive the truth: but seeing it is so, because you will not suffer us to persist in the first, we must of necessity proceed to the other part of our commission. Therefore, I pray you, hearken to what I shall say.'

And forthwith he read the sentence of condemnation, which was written in a long process; the substance of which was, that the said Nicholas Ridley did affirm, maintain, and stubbornly defend certain opinions, assertions, and heresies, contrary to the Word of God, and the received faith of the Church, and could by no means be turned from these heresies. They therefore condemned him as an obstinate heretic, and adjudged him presently, both by word and in deed, to be degraded from the degree of a bishop, from the priesthood, and all the ecclesiastical orders; declaring him, moreover, to be no member of the Church, and therefore they committed him to the secular powers, of them to receive the due punishment according to the temporal laws.

The last examination of Bishop Latimer before the Commissioners
Lincoln: Recant, revoke your errors and turn to the catholic Church.
Latimer: Your lordship often repeats the 'catholic Church', as though I should deny the same. No, my lord, I confess there is a catholic Church, to the determination of which I will stand, but not the church which you call catholic, which ought rather to be termed diabolic. Christ made one oblation and sacrifice for the sins of the whole world, and that a perfect sacrifice; neither needeth there to be, nor can there be, any other propitiatory sacrifice.

Lincoln: Recant, revoke your errors and false assertions.

Latimer: I will not deny my Master, Christ.

The bishop then committed Mr Ridley to the mayor, saying, 'Now he is your prisoner, Mr Mayor.'

Ridley and Latimer's martyrdom, 16th October, 1555

The place for their execution was chosen on the north side of Oxford, in the ditch over against Balliol College; and for fear of any tumult that might arise to hinder the burning of the servants of Christ, the Lord Williams and the householders of the city were commanded by the queen's letters to be prepared to assist if required.

Dr Ridley had on a black gown, furred and faced with foins, such as he used to wear when he was a bishop; a tippet of velvet, furred likewise, about his neck; a velvet night-cap upon his head, with a corner cap; and slippers on his feet. He walked to the stake between the mayor and the alderman.

After him came Mr Latimer, in a poor Bristow frieze frock, much worn, with his buttoned cap and kerchief on his head, and a new long shroud hanging down to his feet. The sight of these two martyrs stirred men's hearts to rue upon them, beholding, on the one hand, the honour they sometimes had, and on the other, the calamity into which they had fallen.

They came to the stake. Dr Ridley, earnestly holding up both his hands, looked towards heaven; then shortly after, seeing Mr Latimer, with a cheerful look he ran to him and embraced him, saying, 'Be of good heart, brother, for God will either assuage the fury of the flame, or else strengthen us to abide it.'

He then went to the stake, and, kneeling down, prayed with great fervour, while Mr Latimer following, kneeled also, and prayed with like earnestness. After this, they arose and conversed together, and, while thus employed, Dr Smith began his sermon from Paul's epistle to the Corinthians, chapter 13: 'If I yield my body to the fire to be burnt, and have not charity, I shall gain nothing thereby.' Strange paradox, that this panegyric on love ... should have been so prostituted on this occasion.

At the conclusion of the sermon, which only lasted a quarter of an hour, Ridley said to Latimer, 'Will you answer, or shall I?'

Mr Latimer said, 'Begin you first, I pray you.'

'I will,' said Dr Ridley.

He then, with Mr Latimer, kneeled to my Lord Williams, the Vice-Chancellor of Oxford, and the other commissioners, who sat upon a form, and said, 'I beseech you, my lord, even for Christ's sake, that I may speak but two or three words.'

And while my lord bent his head to the mayor and Vice-Chancellor, to know whether he might have leave to speak, the bailiffs and Dr

Marshal, the Vice-Chancellor, ran hastily to him, and, with their hands stopping his mouth, said, 'Mr Ridley, if you will revoke your erroneous opinions, you shall not only have liberty so to do, but also your life.'

'Not otherwise?' said Dr Ridley.

'No,' answered Dr Marshal; 'therefore, if you will not do so, there is no remedy: you must suffer for your deserts.'

'Well,' said the martyr, 'so long as the breath is in my body, I will never deny my Lord Christ and his known truth. God's will be done in me.' With that he rose, and said, with a loud voice, 'I commit our cause to Almighty God, who will indifferently judge all.'

To which Mr Latimer added his old saying, 'Well, there is nothing hid but it shall be opened.' They were then commanded to prepare immediately for the stake.

They accordingly obeyed with all meekness. Dr Ridley gave his gown and tippet to his brother-in-law, Mr Shipside, who all the time of his imprisonment, although he was not suffered to come to him, lay there, at his own charges, to provide him necessaries, which he sent him by the sergeant in charge. Some other of his apparel he also gave away; the others the bailiffs took.

He likewise made presents of other small things to gentlemen standing by, divers of whom were weeping pitifully. To Sir Henry Lea he gave a new groat; to my Lord Williams' gentleman, some napkins; some nutmegs, some pieces of ginger, his watch dial, and all that he had about him, he gave to those who stood near. Some plucked the points off his hose, and happy was he who could get the least rag for a remembrance of this good man.

Mr Latimer quietly suffered his keeper to pull off his hose and his other apparel, which was very simple; and being stripped to his shroud, he seemed as comely a person as one could well see.

Then Dr Ridley, standing as yet in his truss, or trousers, said to his brother, 'It were best for me to go in my trousers still.'

'No,' said Mr Latimer, 'it will put you to more pain; and it will do a poor man good.'

Whereunto Dr Ridley said, 'Be it, in the name of God,' and so unlaced himself. Then, being in his shirt, he held up his hand, and said, 'Oh, heavenly Father, I give unto thee most hearty thanks that thou hast called me to be a professor of thee, even unto death. I beseech thee, Lord God, have mercy on this realm of England, and deliver it from all her enemies.'

Then the smith took an iron chain and placed it about both their waists; and as he was knocking in the staple, Dr Ridley took the chain in his hand, and, looking aside to the smith, said, 'Good fellow, knock it in hard, for the flesh will have its course.'

Then Dr Ridley's brother (Shipside) brought him a bag of gunpowder and tied it about his neck. Dr Ridley asked him what it was. He answered,

'Gunpowder.'

Then he said, 'I will take it to be sent of God, therefore I will receive it. And have you any,' said he, 'for my brother?' (meaning Mr Latimer).

'Yea, sir, that I have,' said he.

'Then give it him,' said he, 'in time, lest you come too late.'

So his brother went and carried it to Mr Latimer.

They then brought a lighted faggot, and laid it at Dr Ridley's feet; upon which Mr Latimer said, 'Be of good comfort, Mr Ridley, and play the man! We shall this day light such a candle, by God's grace, in England, as I trust never shall be put out.'

When Dr Ridley saw the fire flaming up towards him, he cried out, with an amazing loud voice, 'Into thy hands, O Lord, I commend my spirit: Lord, receive my spirit!' and continued often to repeat, 'Lord, Lord, receive my spirit!'

Mr Latimer cried as vehemently, 'O Father of heaven, receive my soul!' after which he soon died, seemingly with little pain.

But Dr Ridley, owing to the bad arrangement of the fire (the faggots being green, and piled too high, so that the flames were kept down by the green wood, and burned fiercely beneath), was put to such exquisite pain, that he desired them, for God's sake, to let the fire come to him; which his brother-in-law heard, but did not very well understand; so to rid him out of his pain (for which cause he gave attendance), and not well knowing what he did, in his own sorrow, he heaped faggots upon him, so that he quite covered him, which made the fire so vehement beneath, that it burned all Ridley's lower parts before it touched his upper, and made him struggle under the faggots. Ridley, in his agony, often desired the spectators to let the fire come to him, saying, 'I cannot burn.' Yet in all his torment he did not forget always to call upon God, 'Lord, have mercy upon me!' yet intermingling his cry with 'Let the fire come unto me, I cannot burn;' in which pain he laboured till one of the bystanders pulled the faggots from above with his bill, and where Ridley saw the fire flame up, he leaned himself to that side. As soon as the fire touched the gunpowder, he was seen to stir no more, but burned on the other side, falling down at Mr Latimer's feet, his body being divided.

The dreadful sight filled almost every eye with tears, for some pitied their persons, who thought their souls had no need thereof.

John Foxe (The Book of Martyrs)

William Tyndale (sixteenth-century Bible translator)

During William Tyndale's imprisonment, he wrote a letter which lay buried in the archives of the Council of Brabant for 300 years. It reveals how the great Bible translator's enthusiasm for his work stayed with him, even in his cell. He wrote:

I believe, right worshipful, that you are not unaware of what may have been determined concerning me. Wherefore I beg your lordship, and that by the Lord Jesus that if I am to remain here through the winter, you will request the commissary to have the kindness to send me, from the goods of mine which he has, a warmer cap, for I suffer greatly from cold in the head, and am afflicted by perpetual catarrh, which is much increased in this cell; a warmer coat also, for this which I have is very thin; a piece of cloth, too to patch my leggings. My overcoat is worn out; my shirts also are worn out. He has a woollen shirt, if he will be good enough to send it. I have also with him leggings of thicker cloth to put on above; he has also warmer night-caps. And I ask to be allowed a lamp in the evening; it is indeed wearisome sitting alone in the dark. But most of all I beg and beseech your clemency to be urgent with the commissary, that he will kindly permit me to have the Hebrew Bible, Hebrew grammar and Hebrew dictionary, that I may pass my time in that study. In return may you obtain what you most desire, so only that it be for the salvation of your soul. But if any other decision has been taken concerning me, to be carried out before winter, I will be patient, abiding the will of God to the glory of the grace of my Lord Jesus Christ; whose Spirit (I pray) may ever direct your heart.

W. Tindalus

Tyndale wanted his Hebrew books so that he could finish translating the Old Testament. He had already translated the New Testament – this was the very first translation into English from the Greek original. Tyndale's translation of the Pentateuch (the first five Old Testament books) had been published in 1530, and his translation of the historical books of the Old Testament was ready for publication, so he was keen to finish this work. John Foxe records the events of 6 October 1536 which prevented this: 'Tyndale was brought forth to the place of execution, was there tied to the stake, and then strangled first by the hangman and afterwards by fire consumed, in the morning at the town of Vilvorde, AD 1536; crying thus at the stake with a fervent zeal and a loud voice: "Lord, open the King of England's eyes." '

When the apostle Paul lay in prison in Rome just before the last winter of his life, waiting for his own death sentence, he sent a message to his trusted friend Timothy in Asia Minor: 'Do your best to come to me quickly... When you come, bring the cloak that I left with Carpus at Troas, and my scrolls, especially the parchments' (2 Timothy 4:9, 13). Tyndale asked for his Hebrew Bible; similarly, Paul asked for his scrolls.

MIRACLES

See also **Incarnation**

In his book *Something Beautiful for God* Malcolm Muggeridge writes that in 1969 he travelled to Calcutta to film the work of Mother Teresa. The small team that went with him included Ken Macmillan, a gifted and experienced cameraman.

In Calcutta the Sisters cared for dying people in a room that was badly lit by small windows high in the wall. The camera team had only one small light with them, and in the limited time available it was impossible to light the room adequately. Technically, filming was impossible. Nevertheless, they went ahead, filming both inside the room and in the courtyard outside.

Muggeridge writes: 'In the processed film the part taken inside was bathed in a particularly beautiful soft light, whereas the part taken outside was rather dim and confused.' He adds, 'I am personally persuaded that Ken recorded the first authentic photographic miracle.'

On a subsequent filming trip to the Middle East, Ken Macmillan used some of the same stock of film in a similar bad light, with very poor results.

Muggeridge writes that Mother Teresa's home for the dying is filled with love, and 'this love is luminous.'

In his book *Signs and Wonders* Dr Peter Wagner tries to find out why the Church in China grew so amazingly from 1949 onwards. In this period Chairman Mao expelled all foreign missionaries and executed or exiled to labour camps all Chinese Christian leaders. Thousands of Christians were martyred. Christians were forbidden to meet together and there were very few Bibles. Wagner concludes that 'signs and wonders' played a major role in the growth of the Christian Church in China.

He recounts the story of a woman who worked in a quarry. She was in charge of the work shifts, so whenever she blew her whistle it was the signal for the people to come to the surface from the mines.

One day she was working in her office when she heard a voice calling her by name, telling her that she should blow the whistle to let the workers come up out of the mines. There was still another hour to go before she was supposed to do this, but she repeatedly heard the voice telling her to blow her whistle now. Finally, without checking with the other members of her office, because she thought they would stop her, she blew the whistle. The miners started coming out. No sooner had the last one left the mines than an earthquake caved in several of the shafts. If the workers had still been in the mines, the death toll would have been staggering.

The miners gathered round this girl and asked her why she had blown the whistle early. She had to admit that she was a Christian and that she had just obeyed the voice of God. Hundreds accepted the Lord that day.

Then, at an official enquiry, she gave a powerful testimony and many more families accepted Christ.

MISSION
See also **Angels; Calling; Patience; Protection**
The church exists by mission, as fire exists by burning.
Emil Brunner

Dr Donald Carr was a missionary in Persia (the country now called Iran). When asked how he had received his call to become a missionary, he replied, 'I had no call to stay at home, but I had the command to go.'

Bishop Taylor-Smith changed his mind about a call to go overseas to Sierra Leone, thanks to a visit he made to Westminister Abbey. On David Livingstone's grave he found the words: 'Other sheep I have...' He later recalled: 'I had to ask the Lord three questions: First, who shall bring in these sheep if we do not offer our feet to go? Second, how shall they be brought in, if our hands are not working to bring them in? Third, how shall they hear if our lips do not speak to them?' During World War I he served as Chaplain-General to the Forces.

Jim Elliot (martyred missionary)
Soon after Jim Elliot graduated as a theological student in 1949 he had premonitions that he would die young in God's service. He became convinced that God was calling him to pioneer missionary work in Ecuador. He spent most of 1952 in Quito, Ecuador, learning Spanish and orientating to a new culture. He then went to Shandia and helped to build up a jungle mission station, where he also had to learn a new language so he could speak with the Quichua Indians.

Since his college days Jim had been fascinated by a remote Stone Age tribe in Ecuador known as the Aucas. Jim knew they had a deserved reputation for killing anyone, Indian or white, who dared to intrude into their land. Nevertheless, Jim felt it right to pray especially for these Aucas. While he worked with his new wife Elisabeth among the Quichua Indians, Jim's thoughts often turned to how he might be able to contact the Aucas.

Then, in September 1955, a pilot with Mission Aviation Fellowship named Nate Saint spotted a small Auca settlement while he was flying with Ed McCully. They quickly reported their discovery to Jim Elliot. Ed, Nate and Jim then spent the next three months making weekly flights over the Aucas, dropping gifts of ribbons and cloth on every occasion.

Soon the Aucas would leave their leaf-thatched houses and dug-out canoes and wait for the weekly visit from the air. When the plane circled overhead the Aucas were surprised to hear the men in it shouting in their own language, 'We like you!' and 'We are your friends!'

By late 1955 Ed, Nate and Jim, together with Pete Fleming and Roger Youderian from the Gospel Missionary Union, thought it was time to try and meet up with the Aucas. Nate had found a suitable flat beach on the Curray River where he could land his plane. On 3 January 1956 Nate landed Jim, Ed, Roger and Pete on the beach. There they built a tree house and looked forward to meeting the Aucas from the neighbouring jungle. The plane then flew over the Aucas, and they could hardly believe their ears when they were told in their own language, 'We are on the Curray. Come and see us.' To the delight of the missionaries, three young Aucas – two men and one woman – visited them. The visit seemed to be a total success. They gave them hamburgers and lemonade, and one of the Aucas even went for a ride in the plane. Three days later Nate saw ten Aucas leaving their village and heading for the base on the river. He returned to the other four men with this news.

The five missionaries did not use the guns they had, but were speared to death by these ten Aucas. Their plane was destroyed.

However, the following press release from Wycliffe Bible Translators (June 1992) reports a happy sequel to this tragic story:

When the first translators came to Ecuador and were introduced to the President as people interested in minority groups, they were warned to avoid the notorious Waorani [Auca] Indians. When the President's plane had flown over Waorani territory, they had thrown spears at it. But he was surprised by the bold reply, 'When God opens the door, it will be safe to go.'

Five young men were killed at the hands of the Waorani when they made their first approach. But after much prayer and persistence their confidence was gained, translation began, and a number of them became Christians.

When the President heard that Waoranis (of all people) had become Christians he arranged to visit some of them. His plane landed in a clearing in the jungle, where a group of Waorani men were standing quietly waiting for him. When they were presented to the President they were wide-eyed with astonishment, because he was completely bald! One of them stepped forward with his arm stretched out in front of him. Not knowing quite what was coming, the President backed away, but the man just wanted to rub the top of the President's head!

The President for his part, amazed at the change in the Waorani people, turned to the translator and said, 'Do you really think these people can understand theology?'

'Ask them,' came the wise reply.

So the President addressed one of them, 'What do you know about Jesus?' Immediately the man's eyes lit up and for a good thirty minutes he preached the gospel to the President of the Republic.

Back in the capital, the President summoned his cabinet to meet the translator. 'I was a believer, but I have wandered away from the Truth,' he said. Turning to his cabinet ministers, he asked them, one by one, 'What about you?' After much embarrassment, the President resumed, 'This man will tell you about the power that is transforming the people in our jungle.'

Last month, thirteen people were baptised and the Waorani New Testament was presented to the people. Two of the pastors present were involved in the deaths of the missionaries thirty-six years before. One Waorani leader said in his speech, 'We no longer want to live like those who killed each other and outsiders. We want to live by what God says. Ever since I was a small boy I have heard that we were going to get this book; now we have it.'

MONEY

See also **Greed; Possessions**

The only thing I like about rich people is their money.
Lady Astor

When I was young I thought that money was the most important thing in life; now that I am old I know that it is.
Oscar Wilde

No one is really rich if he can count his money.
Paul Getty

Once, when my mother mentioned an amount and I realized I didn't understand, she had to explain, 'That's like three Mercedes.' Then I understood.
Brooke Shields (supermodel)

I don't wake up for less than $10,000 a day.
Linda Evangelista (supermodel)

Everyone should have enough money to get plastic surgery.
Beverley Johnson (supermodel)

MOTHERS
I learned more about Christianity from my mother than from all the theologians in England.
John Wesley

When he was asked to check a list of the people who had taught him, Winston Churchill said, 'You have omitted to mention the greatest of my teachers – my mother.'

Referring to his Christian mother, who had wept and prayed for him during his years of reckless living, Augustine said in his *Confessions*, 'It is impossible that the son of these tears should perish.'

No man is poor who has a godly mother.
Abraham Lincoln

MUSIC
'Why must the devil have all the best tunes?' This saying can be traced back to Rowland Hill (1744–1833), who said, 'I do not see any good reason why the devil should have all the good tunes.' He was talking about Charles Wesley's practice of putting popular tunes to his new hymns.

General Booth, the founder of the Salvation Army, used this quotation when he was asked why he allowed over 80 Christian hymns, songs and choruses to be set to music-hall tunes.

Music is hateful and intolerable to the devil. I truly believe, and I do not mind saying, that there is no art like music, next to theology. It is the only art, next to theology, that can calm the agitations of the soul, which plainly shows that the devil, the source of anxiety and sadness, flees from the sound of music as he does from religious worship.

That is why the scriptures are full of psalms and hymns, in which praise is given to God. That is why, when we gather round God's throne in heaven, we shall sing his glory. Music is the perfect way to express our

love and devotion to God. It is one of the most magnificent and delightful presents God has given us.
Martin Luther

The Church knew what the psalmist knew: Music praises God. Music is well or better able to praise him than the building of the church and all its decoration; it is the Church's greatest ornament.
Igor Stravinsky

In his book *Bats in the Belfry*, Murray Watts tells of a church organist who 'struggled valiantly' through three hymns. When the vicar whispered a request that he play something more up to date, the organist hissed back that there wasn't anything more up to date, because he was making it up as he went along!

NEIGHBOURS

Many people today show a high degree of irresponsible detachment. Their attitude is the same as that of Cain, who said, 'Am I my brother's keeper?' (Genesis 4:9). A frightening example of this happened in New York on 13 March 1964, as reported in *Life* Magazine:

A decent pretty young woman of 28 called Kitty Genovese was returning home from her job as manager for a bar. It was 3.20 a.m. She had parked her car and was walking the remaining few yards to her apartment, when she was attacked by a man and stabbed. She screamed for help. Several lights went on in the apartment block, and somebody shouted from an upper window, 'Let the girl alone.' The assailant looked up, shrugged his shoulders and walked off. But as the lights went out again and nobody came to her rescue, he returned and stabbed her a second time. At her renewed screams more lights went on, windows were opened and heads looked out. So the man got into his car and drove away. But again, as nobody came to help her, he returned to stab her for the third time and kill her. Not until 3.50 a.m. did the police receive their first telephone call. By then she was dead.

When the police questioned local residents, they found that at least 38 respectable middle-class, law-abiding citizens had heard the woman's screams and had watched her being stabbed, but not one had done anything about it. She had even recognized one witness and called him by name, but he did not reply. Why, the police asked, had these people not come to her aid? Some confessed that they did not know. A housewife said, she 'thought it was a lovers' quarrel'. A man explained without emotion, 'I was tired. I went back to bed.' 'But the word we kept hearing from the witnesses,' said Police Lieutenant Bernard Jacobs, 'was "involved". People told us they just didn't want to get involved.'

NEWS

Tennyson spent one of his holidays with a Methodist family in Lincolnshire. When he arrived he asked his host if she had any news for him. She replied, 'Mr Tennyson, there's only one piece of news that I know – Christ died for all men.' Tennyson said, 'That's old news, and good news, and new news.'

The word 'news' is derived from the initial letters of the four points of the compass: North, East, West, South. News comes from all around us, but the best news comes from above us.

NEWSPAPERS

I would rather exercise than read a newspaper.
Kim Alexis (supermodel)

Samantha Fox used to be a Page 3 Girl in the *Sun* newspaper, but later she became a Christian. This was reported in the *Sun* under the headline, 'My heavenly bod [body] is just for God.'

In an interview with *The Independent* in 1993 the British politician David Mellor said: 'The tabloids are like animals, with their own behavioural patterns. There's no point in complaining about them any more than complaining that lions might eat you. They're trying to run an alternative criminal-justice system without any of the rules of fair play... But there's no point in hating them. I remember talking to John Wakeman, whose wife was killed by the IRA bomb, and he himself was injured. He was sitting one day in the House with his leg up, obviously in pain, and I said, "Don't you feel bitterness towards them?" He said, "Never feel bitter. It means they've won." '

P

PAGANISM

The Emperor Diocletian took counsel and decided to do the things that were unseemly before God, Jesus the Christ; and this is what he did. He made seventy images of gold, and gave unto them the name of 'gods', which they certainly were not. To thirty-five of these he gave names of gods, and to thirty-five the name of goddesses; now the number of his other gods and goddesses amount to one hundred and forty.

And the Emperor Diocletian affixed a decree on the outside of the door of the Palace, wherein it was written thus: 'I, the Emperor Diocletian command that from Romania, in the north, to Pelak, in the south, every man, whether he be a general, or count, or bishop, or elder, or deacon, or reader, or servant, or free man, or soldier, or countryman, shall worship my gods. And any one among these who shall say, "I am a Christian," shall be remembered, and he shall die by the sword. And as for you, O all ye noblemen of high senatorial rank, and officers at court, ye shall give effect to this decree in such a way that every man shall worship my gods; for these are the gods who give us victory in battle, and it is they who are the protectors of you yourselves, and they give strength unto you and unto the whole army. Therefore, he that doth not rise up early in the morning, and come at dawn to me so that we may go into the temple together and offer up sacrifices to the gods, he, I say, that doth not come here shall be cast into the sea, so that all men may know that I am king, and that there is no other king besides me.'

And it came to pass at dawn, on the first day of the month Parmoute, that the Emperor Diocletian, and all his army, and the eparchs, and the generals went into the temple. And the Emperor took his seat upon the throne, and he caused the herald to make a proclamation, saying, 'O all ye Roman people, come ye and offer up sacrifice.' And the Emperor made an altar of silver and a vessel wherein to burn incense of gold; and he made a great pedestal of gold, and he placed it before the altar so that the statue of Apollo might be set upon it. And the Emperor commanded them to bring frankincense, and the finest flour of wheat, and the purest oil, and rare old wine, and pour them out upon the altar whereon was blazing fire. And afterwards they lighted two hundred candles on golden candlesticks, and four hundred candles on silver candlesticks, and two hundred white horses drew his gods into the temple.

And when they had brought his gods into the temple the Emperor Diocletian stood up on his throne, and he lifted his crown off his head, and set it upon the head of the statue of Apollo, and he bowed down and

worshipped it three times, saying, 'Thou art the god who livest, O Apollo, the greatest of the gods, who dost give unto us victory in war.' And after the Emperor had worshipped Apollo, his three fellow Caesars Romanus, Basileides, and Euaios, came and worshipped Apollo also.
E. A. Wallis Budge

PATIENCE

There are three indispensable requirements for a missionary: 1. Patience. 2. Patience. 3. Patience.
Hudson Taylor

PEACE

See **God:** Peace of God; Presence of God

PEOPLE

I have no secret. You haven't learned life's lesson very well if you haven't noticed that you can give the tone or colour, or decide the reaction you want of people in advance. It's unbelievably simple. If you want them to smile, smile first. If you want them to take an interest in you, take an interest in them first. If you want to make them nervous, become nervous yourself. If you want them to shout and raise their voices, raise yours and shout. If you want them to strike you, strike first. It's as simple as that. People will treat you like you treat them. It's no secret. Look about you. You can prove it with the next person you meet.
Winston Churchill

PERSECUTION

See also **Martyrdom; Suffering**
Jesus promised his disciples three things – that they would be completely fearless, absurdly happy and in constant trouble.
G. K. Chesterton

The term 'conspiracy' should not be applied to us but rather to those who plot to foment hatred against decent and worthy people, those who shout for the blood of the innocent and plead forsooth in justification of their hatred the foolish excuse that the Christians are to blame for every public disaster and every misfortune that befalls the people. If the Tiber rises to the walls, if the Nile fails to rise and flood the fields, if the sky withholds

its rain, if there is earthquake or famine or plague, straightaway the cry arises: 'The Christians to the lions!'
Tertullian

In the first century numerous Christians were thrown to the lions because of their faithfulness to Christ. Some other Christians endured a fate which in some ways was even worse. Instead of being condemned to martyrdom they were *damnatus ad metalla*, 'condemned to the mines'. There they experienced indescribable suffering.

Many failed to reach the mines because they first of all had to row their own galley to North Africa under the Roman lash, before being forced to trek across the sun-scorched sands to the Numidian mines. Before they were forced underground into the mines they had their chains shortened so that they could never stand up again, and red-hot irons branded their foreheads. They were then given lamps and hammers and were thrown into the mines, from where they never returned.

Some of these condemned Christians wrote messages in charcoal on the smooth rock, while others wrote out their favourite prayers. Centuries later, when these mines were visited, it was found that one word had been written out again and again: *Vita, Vita, Vita* or 'Life, Life, Life.' One historian, commenting on these inscriptions, described how this word was written in long black lines 'like a flight of swallows chasing one another towards the light.'

These first-century Christians, in the middle of their tortures, experienced at first hand the truth of Paul's words, 'For me, to live is Christ to die is gain.'

A. M. Rosenthal, writing in *The New York Times*, says, 'One of the shocking untold stories of our time, is that more Christians have died this century simply for being Christians than in any century since Christ was born.' Rosenthal accuses the majority of Christian leaders of not speaking out in defence of persecuted Christians.

The persecution of Christians in this century arises from Communism and militant Islam. It is frequently found in Sudan, Pakistan, North Korea, Vietnam, Laos, Egypt, Nigeria, Cuba and Uzbekistan. It is worst in Saudi Arabia, where no religion is allowed except Islam, and in China, where worship or preaching without permission is forbidden.

PERSEVERANCE

In February 1997 Sue Evans-Jones, from Yate, near Bristol, England, passed her driving test. She had been taught by 10 driving instructors over a period of 27 years, and had spent over £20,000 on her 1,800 driving lessons.

A tortoise and a hare had an argument about which of them was the faster, and before they separated they agreed to settle the matter at a particular place at a particular time. The hare was so confident about how fast he could run that he gave no thought to the race with the tortoise. He just lay down in a field and went to sleep. The tortoise was so conscious of his slowness that he kept on going, and did not even stop when he saw the sleeping hare. Eventually the tortoise won the race.

Moral: A naturally gifted person who does not apply himself to a task is often beaten by a plodder.

One of Aesop's fables

The Decca Recording Company turned down the Beatles in 1962, saying, 'We don't like their sound. Groups of guitars are on the way out.' The Beatles were then turned down by other record companies, including Pye, Columbia and HMV.

In 1932, one of the worst years of the Great Depression in America, Charles Darrow, an out-of-work heating engineer in Philadelphia, thought of a way to make some money by giving a few hours of pleasure to other unemployed people. He designed a game in which anybody, after a few throws of the dice, could become a multi-millionaire. When he had finished his invention he took it to Parker Brothers, the games manufacturers, who turned down the game, pointing out that it had 52 fundamental errors. But Darrow did not give up. During the next two years he kept improving his game and pestered Parker Brothers to take it. Eventually, they agreed to see if they could market the game, which quickly became the world's best-selling copyrighted game, *Monopoly*.

When William Carey the missionary was an old man his nephew once asked him if he could one day write his biography. Carey replied, 'If the biographer gives me credit for being a plodder, he will describe me justly. Anything beyond this will be too much. I can plod. I can persevere in any definite pursuit. To this I owe everything.'

Perseverance is the sister of patience, the daughter of constancy, the friend of peace, the cementer of friendships, the bond of harmony and the bulwark of holiness.
Bernard of Clairvaux

Agatha Christie was turned down by 17 publishers before she managed to see her first detective novel published. Dava Sobel was turned down by 10 British publishers before her first novel, *Longitude*, was published. The story about a John Harrison's struggle to invent a chronometer made Sobel into a millionairess in a mere 23 weeks, as her book topped the best-selling lists for half a year.

There must be a beginning to any great matter, but the continuing to the end until it be thoroughly finished yields the true glory.
Francis Drake

All things are possible to him who believes,
yet more to him who hopes,
more still to him who loves,
and most of all to him who practises and perseveres in these three virtues.
Brother Lawrence

PHILOSOPHY

Philosophy has shown itself over and over again to be full of arguments but lacking in conclusions.
Hugh Sylvester

Unintelligible answers to insoluble problems.
Henry Adams

The Chinese philosopher Confucius (551–479 BC) based his teachings on ideas such as loyalty and respect. His most famous saying is: 'What you do not wish done to yourself, do not do to others.'

PLANNING

To fail to plan is knowingly planning to fail.
Author unknown

POLITENESS

In 1942, during World War II, Sir Laurens van der Post, the writer, explorer and conservationist, encountered a group of Japanese soldiers in a jungle clearing in Java. With their bayonets raised, they were about to kill him, but he said, in the highly cultured Japanese he had learned from a friend: 'Would you please excuse me and be so good as to condescend and wait an honourable moment?' This saved his life.

POLITICS

You can't divorce religious belief and public service ... I've never detected any conflict between God's will and my political duty. If you violate one, you violate the other.
Jimmy Carter

While President, I sought to make my administration the most open in history. Secrecy is necessary at times, but this should not be assumed to protect officials from public scrutiny. I maintain my conviction that in our government of the people, for the people, and by the people, the people have the right and the need to know what their government is about.
Jimmy Carter

POSSESSIONS

See also **Greed; Money**
Actress Britt Ekland says she was possessed by her possessions following the break-up of her marriage to Peter Sellers. But in 1997 she changed and commissioned Christie's to auction all the possessions she had held dear when married to Sellers. She even sold off her wedding dress.

POVERTY

See also **Money; Social action**
When Atlanta tidied up its streets for guests at the Olympics, Anita Beatry of the Atlanta Task Force on the Homeless revealed that 9,000 arrests had been made of homeless people in the preceding 12 months. This was four times more than the previous Atlanta record. City officials

had been assisted by a tough new ordinance. The law allowed police to arrest people for 'acting in a manner not usual for law-abiding individuals' in parking lots and garages. Those who had been determined to be acting 'not usual' could be sentenced to up to six months in jail or to a public works project.

POWER

Power tends to corrupt and absolute power corrupts absolutely.
Lord Acton

Unlimited power is apt to corrupt the minds of those who possess it.
William Pitt

PRAYER

There is a story about three men in a boat. No, not the famous three on their trip down the Thames, but another three men in a boat. They were sinking. The first man couldn't pray because he was an atheist. The second man couldn't pray because he couldn't think of any prayers suitable for sinking boats. So the third man prayed, 'We're in a mess, God. Please help us, and we'll never trouble you again.'

A group of local church ministers had met together to study Ephesians 6, and they were just considering the verse, 'Pray at all times' when a maid brought in coffee. So the host turned to the young woman, whom he knew to be a Christian, and asked her what she thought this verse meant.

She said, 'Why, that's exactly what I do each day. When I wash, I think of my sins being washed away. When I light the fire, I think of the bright light that I should be for the Lord Jesus. When I wash the dishes, I think of the kind of utensil I should be for the Lord.'

She was able to teach those ministers something about practising the presence of God in prayer, which no amount of academic knowledge could have taught them.

Pray as if everything depended on God and act as if everything depended on oneself.
Ignatius of Loyola

I asked God for strength that I might achieve;
I was made weak that I might learn humbly to obey.
I asked for help that I might do greater things;
I was given infirmity that I might do better things.
I asked for riches that I might be happy;
I was given poverty that I might be wise.
I asked for all things that I might enjoy life;
I was given life that I might enjoy all things.
I was given nothing I asked for;
But everything that I had hoped for.
Despite myself, my prayers were answered;
I am among all men most richly blessed.
An unknown Confederate soldier

This Scripture pyramid based on Ephesians 3:20 can help us to meditate on prayer:

Ask
All that we ask
All that we ask or think
Above all that we ask or think
Abundantly above all that we ask or think
Able to do abundantly above all that we ask or think.

To work is to pray.
Benedictine proverb

It was my practice to arise at midnight for the purposes of devotion. It seemed to me that God came at the precise time and woke me from sleep in order that I might enjoy him. When I was out of health or greatly fatigued, he did not awaken, but at such times I felt, even in my sleep, a singular possession of God. He loved me so much that he seemed to pervade my being, at a time when I could be only imperfectly conscious of his presence. My sleep is sometimes broken – a sort of half sleep; but my soul seems to be awake enough to know God, when it is hardly capable of knowing anything else.
Madame Guyon

Jonathan Edwards, who has been called 'the greatest theologian on revivals', also published a book which he did not write. It was called *The Life and Diary of David Brainerd.* This book is reckoned by many to have influenced more revivals than any other book. Brainerd was converted at the age of 21 and immediately became a pioneer missionary among the American Indians. After six years of prayer an amazing revival broke out among them. Brainerd spent most of the rest of his short life praying for these Indians, before he died at the age of 29. After he had been a Christian for only three years he wrote these entries in his diary:

In the forenoon, I felt the power of intercession for the advancement of the kingdom of my dear Lord and Saviour in the world; and withal, a most sweet resignation, and even consolation and joy in the thoughts of suffering hardships, distresses, and even death itself, in the promotion of it. In the afternoon God was with me of a truth. Oh, it was a blessed company indeed! My soul was drawn out very much for the world; I think I had more enlargement for sinners, than for the children of God; though I felt as if I could spend my life in cries for both ...

I set apart this day for secret fasting and prayer, to entreat God to direct and bless me with regard to the great work I have in view, of preaching the gospel. Just that night the Lord visited me marvellously in prayer: I think my soul never was in such an agony before. I felt no restraint; for the treasures of divine grace were opened to me. I wrestled for absent friends, for the ingathering of souls, and for the children of God in many distant places. I was in such agony, from sun half an hour high, till near dark, that I was all over wet with sweat; but yet it seemed to me that I had wasted away the day, and had done nothing. Oh, my dear Jesus did sweat blood for poor souls! I longed for compassion towards them.

When God has something very great to accomplish for his church it is his will that there should precede it, the extraordinary prayers of his people. When God is about to accomplish great things for his church, he begins with a remarkable outpouring of his spirit of grace and a desire to pray. If we are not to expect that the devil should go out of a particular person, who is in the grip of bodily possession, without extraordinary prayer, or prayer and fasting; how much less should we expect to have him cast out of the land without it.
Jonathan Edwards

John Ward, a Member of Parliament in the reign of George I, blatantly expressed self-interest in the following prayer:

O Lord, Thou knowest that I have nine houses in the City of London, and that I have lately purchased an estate in Essex. I beseech Thee to preserve the counties of Middlesex and Essex from fires and earthquakes. And, as I have also a mortgage in Hertfordshire, I beg Thee also to have an eye of compassion on that county, and for the rest of the counties Thou mayest deal with them as Thou are pleased. O Lord, enable the banks to answer all their bills, and make all debtors good men. Give prosperous voyage and safe return to the *Mermaid* sloop because I have not insured it. And because Thou hast said, 'The days of the wicked are but short,' I trust that Thou wilt not forget Thy promise, as I have an estate in reversion on the death of the profligate young man, Sir J. L. ... Keep my friends from sinking, preserve me from thieves and housebreakers, and make all my servants so honest and faithful that they may always attend to my interests, and never cheat me out of my property night or day.

It's been said that there is no such thing as unanswered prayer, but that God answers all prayers in one of four ways: firstly, with a 'Yes'; or secondly, with a 'No'; or thirdly, with 'Here is something better'; or fourthly, with 'Wait and see what I am going to do.'

The first is the easiest to receive. We just open our hearts to God and accept what he gives us. The second is often less easy to accept, but we usually realize, as we reflect, that God is being just as loving in giving us a negative reply as he is when he gives us a positive reply. The third answer surprises us, and it is often only later on that we appreciate that it is an answer at all. The fourth answer, 'Wait', is the hardest to cope with. However, a period of waiting is a marvellous opportunity for our trust in God to be deepened.

'Abba' is but a little word, and yet it understands everything. The mouth does not say 'Abba', it is the affection of the heart that speaks in this way. Although I am oppressed with anguish and terror on every side, and seem to be forsaken and utterly cast out of thy presence, yet am I thy child, and thou art my Father. For Christ's sake: I am beloved because of the Beloved.

So this little word 'Father' conceived effectively in the heart, surpasses all the eloquence of Demosthenes, Cicero, and the most eloquent rhetoricians that ever were in the world. This matter is not expressed with words, but with groanings, which groanings cannot be uttered with any words of eloquence, for no tongue can express them.
Martin Luther

One dark night I went into the forest alone to pray. I sat upon a rock. There I laid before God my deep needs and begged his help. After a while I saw a poor man come towards me. I thought he was approaching me to beg some kind of relief because he was hungry and cold.

'I am a poor man, too,' I said to him. 'I have nothing at all but this blanket. You'd better go into the local village and get help there.' Then, as I was still in the middle of speaking, he flashed like lightning, showering drops of blessing, and disappeared immediately. What a bitter disappointment! It was clear to me, too late, that this had been my beloved Master. He came not to beg from a poor wretch like me, but to bless and enrich me. I remained there weeping. With what sorrow I regretted my utter stupidity and lack of insight!
Sundar Singh

PREACHING
See also **Bishops**
A good preacher should have these qualities and virtues:
1. He should teach systematically.
2. He should have a ready wit.
3. He should be eloquent.
4. He should have a good voice.
5. A good memory.
6. He should know when to stop.
7. He should be sure of his doctrine.
8. He should go out and grapple with body and blood, wealth and honour, in the word.
9. He should let himself be mocked and jeered at by everybody.
Martin Luther

Charles Simeon, Dean of King's College and Vicar of Holy Trinity, Cambridge at the beginning of the nineteenth century, endeavoured to follow Paul's advice in all his preaching and teaching. A tablet on the south wall of the church commemorates him as one 'who, whether as the ground of his own hopes or as the subject of all his ministrations determined to know nothing but Jesus Christ and him crucified.'

A reporter once asked Billy Graham, 'Why did you become an evangelist?' 'Let me ask you a question,' replied Billy Graham. 'Suppose I discovered a chemical which would make any person radiant and happy, giving meaning to his life here, and assure him of eternal life hereafter? Then suppose that I decided to keep that secret to myself. Wouldn't you say:

"Billy, you're a criminal"? If I didn't know that faith in Christ is vital, transforming, that it gives direction to life and makes life worth living, I'd go back to my little North Carolina farm and spend the rest of my days tilling the soil. But I have seen too many lives untangled and rehabilitated, too many homes reconstructed, too many people find peace and joy through simple, humble confession and faith in Christ, ever to doubt that he is the answer. I am an evangelist for the same reason that the apostle Paul was: "Woe unto me, if I preach not the gospel." '

'Comfort the afflicted, and afflict the comfortable.' This saying has been applied to the role of the preacher, but was probably first used with reference to the duty of newspapers. The former Archbishop of Canterbury, Michael Ramsey, adapted this saying as follows: 'The duty of the church is to comfort the disturbed and to disturb the comfortable.'

I simply taught, preached, wrote God's word: otherwise I did nothing. And then, while I slept, or drank Wittenberg beer with my friend Philip or my friend Amsdorf, the word so greatly weakened the papacy that no prince or emperor ever inflicted such damage upon it. I did nothing. The word did it all.
Martin Luther

In the United States the vocabulary of an average person is 600 words, whereas that of the average preacher is 5,000 words. So the average person in the pew does not know what the man in the pulpit is saying. That's why I fight to keep it simple.
Billy Graham

A preacher should have the skill to teach the unlearned simply, roundly and plainly; for teaching is more important than exhorting. When I preach I regard neither doctors nor magistrates, of whom I have about forty in the congregation. I have all my eyes on the servant maids and the children. And if the learned men are not well pleased with what they hear, well, the door is open.
Martin Luther

Martyn Lloyd-Jones recounts how he led a university mission at Oxford in 1941. He was invited to preach at the first service of the mission in St

Mary's Church, from the pulpit where John Henry Newman (later Cardinal Newman) had regularly preached. After the service the students were invited to ask questions. The room was packed, and the first question came from a law student who was also a leading light in the famous Oxford University Union Debating Society. He said, 'Your sermon could equally well have been delivered to a congregation of farm labourers.' He sat down to a burst of laughter and applause.

Lloyd-Jones replied, 'I do not see your difficulty. For while you may regard me as a heretic, I have always thought of undergraduates and indeed graduates of Oxford University as being just ordinary common human clay and miserable sinners like everyone else. I hold the view that your needs are precisely the same as those of the agricultural labourer or anyone else. I preached as I did quite deliberately.'

PREJUDICE
See also **Racial prejudice and injustice**
A student once went up to a well-known evangelist and said, 'I've made up my mind. Don't confuse me with facts!'

There was once a man who thought he was dead. Nothing that his parents, friends, doctors or psychiatrists could do or say could persuade him otherwise. One psychiatrist, however, worked out a plan of action. After they had studied a medical textbook together he managed to convince the man of one simple fact: dead men do not bleed. 'Yes, I agree,' said the man. 'Dead men do not bleed.' Whereupon the psychiatrist plunged a small knife into the man's arm, and the blood started to flow. The man looked at his arm, his face white with astonishment and horror. 'Goodness me!' he said. 'Dead men *do* bleed after all!'

PRIDE
The mice and the weasels were at war, and the mice were always coming off worse. The mice held a meeting in which they concluded that their defeats were due to lack of leadership. So they appointed from their ranks some mice to be generals. These generals, to make sure that they could be distinguished from the rest of the mice, made horns and attached them to their heads.

In the next battle between the mice and the weasels the whole mice army was routed and had to flee. All the mice reached their holes safely, except for the generals, who, unable to get into their holes because of their horns, were seized and eaten.

Moral: Vainglory is often the cause of misfortune.
One of Aesop's fables

A cock which had come off worst in a fight with his rival for the affections of the hens went and hid himself in a dark corner. Meanwhile, the victor climbed on to a high wall where he crowed at the top of his voice. Without any warning, an eagle swooped down and snatched him up. The other cock was kept safe in his hiding place and was now able to continue wooing the hens without any fear of being interrupted.

Moral: This story shows how God resists the proud but gives grace to the humble.
One of Aesop's fables

PROCRASTINATION
See also **Starting**

When, as a child, I laughed and wept,
Time crept.
When, as a youth, I dreamed and talked,
Time walked.
What I became a full-grown man,
Time ran.
And later, as I older grew,
Time flew.
Soon I shall find, while travelling on,
Time gone.
Will Christ have saved my soul by then?
Amen.
Inscription on a clock in Chester Cathedral

Have you heard the story of the three devils?

Three devils were having a chat with the chief devil, Satan, and they were hatching a plot on how to ruin mankind. The first said, 'Why don't we try and make them believe that there is no God?'

'That will be no good,' said Satan. 'All they have to do is look at the beautiful world, and they can't help but believe a creator God is responsible for it all.'

'Why don't we make them believe that hell does not exist?' suggested the second devil.

'That won't do,' replied Satan. 'Too many of them are living in hell as it is.'

'Well,' said the third devil. 'Why don't we convince them that there is no hurry?'

'Excellent,' said Satan. 'You go and do that. Tell them that there is no hurry.'

They say that procrastination is the thief of time, but it is also the thief of eternity.

PROPHETIC MESSAGES

I was walking with several friends, I lifted up my head, and saw three steeple-house spires, and they struck at my life. I asked them what place that was? They said, 'Lichfield.' Immediately the word of the Lord came to me, that I must go there. Being come to the house we were going to, I wished the friends to walk into the house, saying nothing to them of whither I was to go. As soon as they were gone I stept away, and went by my eye over hedge and ditch till I came within a mile of Lichfield; where, in a great field, shepherds were keeping their sheep.

Then was I commanded by the Lord to pull off my shoes. I stood still, for it was winter: but the word of the Lord was like a fire in me. So I put off my shoes and left them with the shepherds; and the poor shepherds trembled, and were astonished. Then I walked on about a mile, and as soon as I was got within the city, the word of the Lord came to me again, saying: Cry, 'Wo, to the bloody city of Lichfield!' So I went up and down the streets, crying with a loud voice, 'Wo to the bloody city of Lichfield!' It being market day, I went into the market-place, and to and fro in the several parts of it, and made stands, crying as before, 'Wo to the bloody city of Lichfield!'

And no one laid hands on me. As I went thus crying through the streets, there seemed to me to be a channel of blood running down the streets, and the market-place appeared like a pool of blood. When I had declared what was upon me, and felt myself clear, I went out of the town in peace; and returning to the shepherds gave them some money, and took my shoes of them again. But the fire of the Lord was so on my feet, and all over me, that I did not matter to put on my shoes again, and was at a stand whether I should or no, till I felt freedom from the Lord so to do: then, after I had washed my feet, I put on my shoes again.

After this a deep consideration came upon me, for what reason I should be sent to cry against that city, and call it 'The bloody city!' For though the parliament had the minister one while, and the king another, and much blood had been shed in the town during the wars between them, yet there was not more than had befallen many other places. But afterwards I came to understand, that in the Emperor Diocletian's time a thousand Christians were martyred in Lichfield. So I was to go, without

my shoes, through the channel of their blood, and into the pool of their blood in the market-place, that I might raise up the memorial of the blood of those martyrs, which had been shed above a thousand years before, and lay cold in their streets. So the sense of this blood was upon me, and I obeyed the word of the Lord.
John Fox (Journal)

PROTECTION

At one time Mary Slessor had been too frightened to cross a field with a cow in it, but when she became a missionary she had to travel alone through the African countryside, which was infested with dangerous animals. She wrote: 'I did not use to believe the story of Daniel in the lions' den until I had to take some of these awful marches, and then I knew it was true, and that it was written for my comfort. Many a time I walked along praying, "O God of Daniel, shut their mouths", and he did.'

PROVIDENCE

Martin Rinkart was a pastor at Eilenberg in Saxony during the Thirty Years' War (1618–48). Because Eilenberg was a walled city it became a severely overcrowded refuge for political and military fugitives from far and near. As a result, the city suffered from famine and disease. In 1637 a great plague swept through the area, resulting in the death of 8,000 people, including Rinkart's wife. By that time he was the only minister left in Eilenberg, as all the others had either died or fled. By himself, Rinkart conducted burial services for 4,480 people, sometimes as many as 40 or 50 in a single day.

During the closing years of the war Eilenberg was overrun or besieged three times, once by the Austrian army and twice by the Swedes. On one occasion the Swedish general demanded a payment of 30,000 thalers from the people left in the town. Rinkart acted as an intermediary, pleading that the impoverished city could not meet such a levy. However, his plea was turned down. Turning to his companions, the pastor said, 'Come, my children, we can find no mercy with man; let us take refuge with God.' On his knees he led the people of the town in a fervent prayer and in the singing of one of their popular hymns, 'When in the hour of utmost need'. The Swedish commander was so moved that he reduced the levy to 1,350 thalers.

We may wonder why such dramatic experiences and horrific hardships are not reflected in Rinkart's famous hymn, 'Now thank we all our God'. Had the good pastor seen so much stark tragedy that he had become insensitive to human needs and problems? No. He simply believed that God's providence is always good, no matter how much we are tempted to doubt it.

In Wolverhampton, England, in July 1996 a nursery teacher named Lisa Potts was scarred for life as she protected the children from a machete-wielding maniac. She suffered injuries to her back, her right hand and her head, and four tendons in her left arm were severed, leaving her with permanent damage. She still suffers from nightmares and flashbacks about that indescribable day. 'But, it hasn't shaken my faith in God,' says Lisa. She has a firm belief that she was 'meant to be in that playground on that day.'

RACIAL PREJUDICE

When Tiger Woods won the 1997 US Master, Golf tournament at the Augusta National Club he broke many records. Aged 21, he became the youngest person to win the title. His 12-stroke lead was a record. He also set a course record with his 18 under par over the 4 rounds. He was the first black person to win any of the four major US golf competitions (Woods is part African-American, part Cherokee, part Thai and part Chinese). Six years ago the Augusta National Golf Club had no ethnic minority members.

In 1997 Marlon Brando received a bad press for his off-hand remark about Hollywood being 'run by Jews'. The comment led to a charge of anti-Semitism. His star on Hollywood's Walk of Fame was defaced by a swastika. He quickly apologized publicly for his remark.

Dr Martin Luther King, champion of civil rights for American blacks, explained his non-violent campaign against injustice in these words:

Our aim must be never to defeat or humiliate the white man, but to win his friendship and understanding. We must come to see that the end we seek is a society at peace with itself, a society that can live with its conscience. That will be a day not of the white man, not of the black man. That will be the day of man as man.

In December 1964 he received the Nobel Peace Prize, presented by King Olav of Norway, in recognition of his tireless campaign against oppression and prejudice.

In 1968 black dustmen had been on strike in Memphis for a week, and Martin Luther King went there to orchestrate a massive non-violent protest. Dr King was being put under great pressure from some other black leaders like Stokely Carmichael because of his avowedly non-violent approach to gaining simple justice for American blacks. He spoke at a pre-march rally on 3 April in which he made clear exactly what he supported in this unequal struggle. He also referred to the numerous threats of violence that he had received, some threatening his life. He said quite openly that he had been warned not to go to Memphis if he wanted to stay alive. He ended his last recorded public speech with these words:

And then I got into Memphis and some began to talk about the threats of what would happen to me from some of our sick white brothers. But I don't know what will happen now. We've got some difficult days ahead. But it really doesn't matter with me now. Because I've been to the mountain-top and I don't mind. Like anybody, I would like to live a long life; longevity has its place, but I'm not concerned about that now. I just want to do God's will, and he's allowed me to go up to the mountain. And I've looked over and I've seen the Promised Land. I may not get there with you, but I want you to know tonight that we as a people will get to the Promised Land. So I'm happy tonight. I'm not fearing any man. Mine eyes have seen the glory of the coming of the Lord.

Dr King was taking a short break the following morning on the balcony of the Lorraine Motel, where he was engaged in a conference. As he turned to return to his room, the assassin's bullet rang out, making a direct, deadly hit on Dr King's face. In vain the dying, 39-year-old Dr King was rushed by ambulance to St Joseph's Hospital, but he never regained consciousness.

On hearing the news, President Johnson said to the American nation on television, 'I ask every citizen to reject the blind violence that has struck Dr King.' On Dr King's tombstone are inscribed the words that he spoke on the famous march on Washington in August 1963:

FREE AT LAST,
FREE AT LAST
THANK GOD ALMIGHTY
I'M FREE AT LAST.

In his Christmas Eve broadcast, shortly before he was assassinated, Martin Luther King outlined his vision for humanity:

I still have a dream this morning that one day every Negro in this country, every coloured person in the world, will be judged on the basis of the content of his character rather than the colour of his skin, and every man will respect the dignity and worth of human personality.

I still have a dream today that one day the idle industries of Appalachia will be revitalized and the empty stomachs of Mississippi will be filled, and brotherhood will be more than a few words at the end of a prayer, but rather the first item on every legislative agenda.

I still have a dream today that one day justice will roll down like water, and righteousness like a mighty stream.

I still have a dream today that in all of our state houses and city halls men will be elected to go there who will do justly, and love mercy and live humbly with their God.

I still have a dream today that one day war will come to an end, that men will beat their swords into ploughshares and their spears into pruning hooks, that nations will no longer rise up against nations, neither will they study war any more.

I still have a dream that with this faith we shall be able to adjourn the councils of despair and bring new light into the dark chambers of pessimism. With this faith we will be able to speed up the day when there will be peace on earth and goodwill toward men. It will be a glorious day, the morning stars will sing together, and the sons of God will shout for joy.

RAINBOWS

My heart leaps up when I behold
A rainbow in the sky.
William Wordsworth

RANSOM

During the Crusades King Richard the Lionheart was captured and a price was set for his freedom. Taxes were levied on the English people. As soon as the ransom price was paid, King Richard was set free. When Jesus Christ died on the cross he paid the ransom so that we could be set free. As Mrs Alexander's hymn puts it:

There was no other good enough
To pay the price of sin;
He only could unlock the gate
Of heaven, and let us in.

In World War II Peter was a Dutch resistance leader. The Germans were delighted when they managed to arrest him, but they were furious when he was subsequently rescued by his own people. The Germans were quick to react. The following morning they seized three other Dutchmen and announced that they would be killed unless Peter was handed over to them by sunset. Sunset came and went. The Resistance Movement refused to hand over Peter. The three hostages were shot.

Peter was never the same again. The fact that other people had died in his place made him redouble his efforts. He dedicated himself more passionately than ever to work for the cause of freedom.

REDEMPTION

In the days of the slave trade in America there was a slave market in New Orleans. Two men strolled in and watched a young man being sold by the auctioneer. All his good points were shown off, as if he were a racehorse. One of these men had recently lost a son of about the same age as this young African who was being sold, and his heart went out to him. So he joined in the bidding, and eventually bought the young man for a high price. He called for the blacksmith, saying, 'Strike off his fetters! I have bought him, and I will make him a free man!'

The chains were struck off the slave's legs, and he, throwing his arms in the air, and with tears running down his cheeks, cried out, 'He's redeemed me! He's redeemed me! I'll follow him and serve him to the end of my life!'

There's a story about a crofter's son who lived in one of the most remote westerly isles of Scotland. This teenager spent the whole of one winter making a model sailing boat. On the first bright day of spring he took his precious craft down to the water's edge for its launch. He lowered it gently and lovingly into the sea. He had shaped the hull so well that the boat was perfectly balanced. He had set the sails so well that the craft was immediately taken out of his reach by a sudden breeze. All he could do was watch his beautiful boat sail out to sea.

The next time he saw his boat it was on sale in a second-hand shop in a neighbouring village. The fisherman who owned the shop told him that its price was five pounds. He was determined to raise the money. So he spent the next few months saving up all his pocket money and doing as many odd jobs as possible. He then went in and bought his boat. On the way out, clutching his boat, he was heard to say, 'You're twice mine. I made you and I bought you!'

REFUGEES

See also **Cruelty**

Eleanor Roosevelt (1884–1962), the wife of US President Franklin D. Roosevelt, campaigned for refugees after World War II and helped to ensure that they would not be forgotten when the UN Charter was written. She wrote: 'If civilization is to survive, we must cultivate the science of human relationships – the ability of all people of all kinds to live together and work together in the same world, at peace.'

REGENERATION
See also **Transformation**

At one of the weekly tea-parties which the famous preacher Charles Simeon used to hold in Cambridge he was asked: 'What, Sir, do you consider the principal mark of regeneration?' He answered: 'The very first and indispensable sign is self-loathing. Nothing short of this can be seen as an evidence of a real change. I want to see more of this humble, contrite, broken spirit among us. Give me to be with a broken-hearted Christian, as I prefer his society to that of all the rest. Were I now addressing to you my dying words, I should say nothing else but what I have just said. Try to live in this spirit of self-abhorrence, and let it habitually mark your life and conduct.'

REPENTANCE

A French admiral was defeated in a sea battle by Nelson. He was brought to Nelson's quarter-deck. He strode forward, with his arm outstretched, as if he were about to greet a friend and equal. Nelson turned his back on him, saying, 'Sir, I want your sword first.' Nelson wanted the admiral to willingly lay down his sword – his symbol of defiance – before him. Only then could there be any talk of friendship between them.

Similarly, Jesus says to us, 'Repent, turn from your sins as the first step. Then you will enjoy my friendship.'

REST

You have created us for yourself, and our heart cannot be stilled until it finds rest in you.
Augustine

RETRIBUTION

The noblest form of retribution is not to become like your enemies.
Marcus Aurelius

REVIVAL
Twenty-four hindrances to revival

A revival is a work of God, and so is a crop of wheat; and God is as much dependent on the use of means in one case as in the other. And therefore a revival is as liable to be injured as a wheat field.

1. A revival will stop whenever the church believe it is going to cease. The church are the instruments with which God carries on this work. Nothing is more fatal to a revival than for its friends to predict that it is going to stop.
2. A revival will cease when Christians consent that it should cease.
3. A revival will cease when Christians become mechanical in their attempts to promote it.
4. A revival will cease whenever Christians get the idea that the work will go on without their aid. The church are co-workers with God in promoting a revival.
5. The work will cease when the church prefer to attend to their own concerns rather than God's business.
6. When Christians get proud of their great revival, it will cease.
7. The revival will stop when the church gets exhausted by labour ... [i.e. when Christians] break up all their habits of living, neglect to eat and sleep at the proper hours ... so that they overdo their bodies, and ... become exhausted...
8. A revival will cease when the church begin to speculate about abstract doctrines, which have nothing to do with practice.
9. When Christians begin to proselytize from other Christian denominations.
10. When Christians refuse to render to the Lord according to the benefits received. God gives people up if they show a niggardly spirit.
11. When the church, in any way, grieve the Holy Spirit: (a) When they do not feel their dependence on the Spirit. (b) The Spirit may be grieved by a spirit of boasting of the revival. (c) The Spirit may be grieved by saying or publishing things that are calculated to undervalue the work of God.
12. A revival may be expected to cease when Christians lose the Spirit of brotherly love.
13. A revival will decline and cease, unless Christians are frequently reconverted. By this I mean, that Christians, in order to keep in the spirit of a revival, commonly need to be frequently convicted, and humbled, and broken down before God, and reconverted...
14. A revival cannot continue when Christians will not practise self-denial.
15. A revival will be stopped by controversies about new measures.
16. Revivals can be put down by the continued opposition of the old school, combined with a bad spirit in the new school.
17. Any diversion of the public mind will hinder a revival. Any thing that succeeds in diverting public attention, will put a stop to revival.
18. Resistance to the temperance reformation will put a stop to revivals in a church.

19. Revivals are hindered when ministers and churches take wrong ground in regard to any question involving human rights, such as the subject of slavery.
20. Another thing that hinders revivals is neglecting the claims of missions.
21. When a church rejects the calls of God upon them for educating young men for the ministry, they will hinder and destroy a revival...
22. Slandering revivals will often put them down...
23. Ecclesiastical difficulties are calculated to grieve away the Spirit, and destroy revivals...
24. Another thing by which revivals may be hindered, is censoriousness on either side, and especially in those who have been engaged in carrying forward a revival. The greatest hindrance to an universal Revival of the work of God, is the divided state of the church of Christ.

Charles Finney

Howel Harris, a Welsh revival preacher, gave this description of his conversion to Christ, which took place on 18 June 1735:

I felt suddenly my heart melting within me, like wax before the fire, with love to God my Saviour. I felt not only love and peace, but also a longing to be dissolved and to be with Christ; and there was a cry in my inmost soul, with which I was totally unacquainted before, it was this – 'Abba, Father; Abba, Father!' I could not help calling God *my* Father; I knew that I was his child, and that he loved me; my soul being filled and satiated, crying, 'It is enough – I am satisfied; give me strength, and I will follow thee through fire and water.'

Satan can counterfeit all the saving operations and graces of the Spirit of God.

Jonathan Edwards

When asked, 'How do you have a revival?' the famous Victorian preacher Gypsy Smith replied, 'Kneel down and with a piece of chalk draw a complete circle all around you – and pray to God to send a revival on everything inside the circle. Stay there until he answers, and you will have revival.'

RIGHTEOUSNESS

Rabbi Simlai, who lived in the third century BC, said Moses gave 365 prohibitions, one for each day of the year, and 248 positive commands, one for each bone in our bodies. David, in Psalm 15, reduced the commands to a mere eleven; Isaiah 33:14–15 made them six; Micah 6:8 reduced them to three; and Habakkuk reduced them all to just one: 'The just shall live by faith.'

SACRIFICE

See also **Jesus Christ:** Jesus our sacrifice

The apocryphal story behind Albrecht Durer's famous *Praying Hands* etching comes from the 1490s. Two friends, Albrecht and Franz, lived and worked together and trained to be artists in their spare time. But their manual work did not provide enough money for them to train properly. They eventually decided to cast lots to see which of them should carry on working, so that the other could be supported at art school. Albrecht won and went to school, while Franz worked even longer hours to provide the money.

Albrecht eventually returned to Franz. Now that Albrecht had become a successful artist, Franz too could go to art school. But Albrecht was heart-broken to discover that Franz's hands had been ruined for ever by the heavy manual work he had undertaken. Franz would now never be able to become an artist. He had given up his own artistic life so that his friend might succeed as an artist.

Albrecht came across Franz praying on his knees one day. His gnarled hands were clasped together. Albrecht quickly sketched his friend's hands, which are now known as the *Praying Hands*. They symbolize the truth that friendship and prayer belong together. We know that the Person to whom we pray has pierced hands.

'I am just going outside, and I may be some time,' were the last words of Captain Lawrence Oates, a member of Captain Scott's expedition to reach the South Pole. They set out on 24 October 1911 with motor sledges, ponies and dogs. The motors broke down, and the ponies and dogs had to be returned. Seven out of the team of eleven men also went back.

Eventually, after 81 days, and pulling their three sledges, five men reached the Pole, only to find that the Norwegians had got there a month earlier. On the return journey they had to endure atrocious weather. Evans died on 17 February. Food and supplies were low. Oates was suffering from gangrene in his feet, frostbite in his hands and scurvy, and he knew he would be the next to die. On 17 March, with little strength left, he crawled out of his tent into a blizzard and did not come back, since he did not want to slow down his companions. The remaining three men struggled on for another 10 miles, before being trapped by another blizzard. There was nothing more they could do. They died only 11 miles from their destination.

Today Eyam is a small, quiet village high in the Derbyshire hills. In the early seventeenth century there were lead works nearby, and Eyam was a prosperous and busy place.

In the 1660s a parcel of cloth was sent from plague-ridden London to the tailor in Eyam. To the horror of the village, the tailor fell ill with the severest form of the plague, dying the same day.

Mr Mompesson, the rector of the parish, wrote to London for information about medical treatment and medicines. He also wrote to the local Lord, the Earl of Devonshire at Chatsworth House. He said that no one would leave the village, and in return he asked the Earl to arrange for food and medicine to be left at specified places and times in the hills around the village. This would be collected by the people of Eyam, and money would be left. He said that all communication with anyone outside the village would be by letter, and suggested that these letters, together with the money, should be fumigated or washed with vinegar before anyone touched them. The Earl agreed.

Mompesson told the people of Eyam of his plan. He said that no one could stop any villager from fleeing, but those who left would most certainly carry the plague with them, which would be selfish and cruel. As far as we know, every villager chose to stay within the village.

The young rector and his wife worked day and night to nurse and care for the sick. For seven months the plague raged in the village, and 259 people died, including the rector's wife. But there was not a single case of the plague in any village around Eyam.

Ernest Gordon's book *Miracle on the River Kwai* tells one of the most wonderful stories of World War II. It is a factual account of life in a labour camp in Thailand where Japanese soldiers forced Allied prisoners of war to build a railway bridge. The appalling conditions there led the prisoners to live by the law of the jungle. They even stole each other's few possessions. Then what the writer describes as a 'miracle' took place.

The camp was revolutionized by the death of Angus, a very strong man. Angus' friend became ill, and it became obvious to everyone, except Angus, that his friend would die. Angus did everything he could to help his friend live. His friend's blanket was stolen from him, so Angus gave him his own. Angus collected all his meals as usual, but instead of eating them himself, he took the meagre rations to his friend and stood over him until he ate them. Being such a huge man made it doubly hard for Angus to go without food. Then, one day, just as Angus' friend was on the road to recovery, Angus died. The doctor said Angus died of starvation, complicated by exhaustion.

At Angus' funeral they read the words, 'Greater love has no one than this, that he lay down his life for his friends.' Ernest Gordon had this incident in mind when he wrote:

Our regeneration, sparked by conspicuous acts of self-sacrifice, had begun... We were seeing for ourselves the sharp contrast between the forces that made for life and those that made for death. Selfishness, hatred, envy, jealousy, greed, self-indulgence, laziness and pride were all anti-life. Love, heroism, self-sacrifice, sympathy, mercy, integrity and creative faith, on the other hand, were the essence of life, turning mere existence into living in its truest sense. These were the gifts of God to men.

The Belgian flag (a tricolour of black, red and gold) was chosen to represent a definite belief. The phrase *De la nuit au jour par le sang* expresses its exact meaning: 'Through blood we passed through the black night to the golden day.' The flag stands as a perpetual reminder to those who sacrificed their lives so that Belgium could be a free country.

SAINTS

The saint is a saint because he received the Holy Spirit, who took up his abode with him and inwardly married himself to the soul.
Abraham Kuyper

Sir Charles Halle, after whom the Halle Orchestra was named, was one of the great pianists of the nineteenth century. He became particularly famous for the way he played and interpreted Beethoven. He was not noted for any showy or spectacular concerts. In a review of one of his concerts in 1888 George Bernard Shaw wrote: 'The secret is that he gives you as little as possible of Halle and as much as possible of Beethoven.'

The Puritan theologian James Denny gave similar advice to preachers when he wrote: 'No preacher can at one and the same time give the impression that he is clever and that Jesus is great and wonderful.'

You may know the story about the little girl who found herself in church for the very first time. She was transfixed by the stained-glass windows. She whispered to her mum, 'Who are the people in the windows?' Her mother did not want to have a lengthy conversation in the middle of the service, so she just replied, 'They're saints.'

In the afternoon the girl went with her mother to visit a very elderly lady. She lived on her own and was very poor, but was the happiest person the girl had ever met. As they walked away from the house, the girl's mum said, 'Old Mrs Brown is a saint, if ever there was one.'

Now this posed a problem in the girl's mind. She had been told two things: the people in the stained-glass windows were saints, and old Mrs Brown was a saint. The girl failed to see the link between the two. Then she puzzled it out and declared, 'Mummy, I know what a saint is.'

'Tell me,' her mum replied.

'A saint is a person who lets the light shine through,' was the wonderful answer.

SALVATION

See also **Conversion; Jesus Christ; Ransom; Redemption**

When I was a student at Oxford I was punting on the river and fell head first into the water. It was a terrifying experience because the thick weeds entangled my legs and arms and I was out of my depth. I was afraid that I was going to drown because I could not reach the shore.

Imagine the possible reaction of some of my undergraduate friends in the boat. Some of them might have said: 'Don't worry, Jim, you'll be all right. You can get out if you only try. Keep on struggling!' Others might have said, 'I'd really like to help you. But, you see, I have a problem with my conscience. I can't interfere with other people's free will. But I can give you a quick lesson on how to swim, if that'll help.'

These two possible responses represent two views about Christian salvation, that have been held through the centuries. The first goes by the name of Pelagianism. Humankind has the natural ability to save itself, if only they will keep working at it. It is an example of the White Queen, telling Alice that you can believe it if only you practice more.

The second response goes under the name of Arminianism. 'I'll help you up to a point, but there are limits about how much even God will help us humans.' It is the White Queen once more, offering advice on how to hold your breath and shut your eyes. Both of these ways of viewing salvation are essentially saying, 'If you try harder, you will be saved. It's all up to you. You can make it through your own efforts.'

But I still had my problem. I was drowning. I wasn't able to get myself out of this difficulty, no matter how hard I tried. I felt like Alice because it was no use trying because 'I just can't believe impossible things.' Was anybody going to help me in my predicament? You can imagine my delight and relief when one of my friends, who was neither an Arminian nor a Pelagian, dived into the river. One of his friends was heard to murmur, 'He can do that because he's a Calvinist.' He untangled me from the weeds, overcame my feeble struggles, brought me to the river bank and started artificial respiration. That is what I call a rescue.

Jim Packer

A Red Indian was once asked by an Englishman why he loved Christ so much. The Indian didn't reply with words, but gathered a few handfuls of dry leaves and made a circle of them. He then placed a worm in the middle of the circle and set light to the leaves. Immediately there was a circle of fire surrounding the worm. Then the Indian removed the worm from the circle. 'That's what Jesus Christ did for me,' said the Indian. 'He rescued me. That's why I love him so much.'

One thief on the cross was saved, that none should despair; and only one, that none should presume.
J. C. Ryle

SAMARITANS

In 1936 an Anglican priest named Chad Varah was asked to take the funeral of a 13-year-old girl. He found out that when her first period had started she had thought that she was suffering from a dreadful illness. With no one to talk to and terribly afraid, she had killed herself. Varah said in his heart, 'Little girl, I never knew you, but you have changed my life.' He decided to take every opportunity to talk to young people about their problems.

Some time later Varah heard that in London alone an average of three people committed suicide every day. How could he offer help to people like this? The quickest way would be for them to phone him. But to embark on such a work would take considerable time, and he was already very busy with a church, hospital work and writing. Then in 1953 St Stephens in London – a city church with relatively few parishioners – invited him to be their rector. He decided to take the job, and set about organizing a telephone help-line in a room in the church.

In October 1953 he rang the local telephone exchange to see if he could be given a telephone number that would be easy for people to remember – preferably a number with a 9 in it, because of the familiarity of 999. He said that if possible he would like Mansion House 9000. The supervisor said she thought most of the easy numbers would already be taken, but she offered to find out, and she asked him for his present number. Varah rubbed the dirt and dust from the dial, and found that he already had the number Mansion House 9000!

In 1996 there were over 200 branches of the Samaritans in the United Kingdom and Ireland, staffed by over 2,000 helpers.

In an article in *The Reader's Digest* Valerie Groves writes that it was the novelist Monica Dickens who brought the Samaritans to America. Dickens became a Samaritan herself after spending time with the Samaritans in England while researching for her book *The Listeners*. The Samaritan way of befriending, she said, 'is so simple, so direct, and so purely human that it can work anywhere in the world.' In 1974 the first branch opened in a church crypt in Boston.

SANCTIFICATION

Sanctification is glory begun. Glory is sanctification completed.
F. F. Bruce

Martyn Lloyd-Jones believed that the phrase 'the day of evil' in Ephesians 6:13 means those special occasions when the devil seems to be let loose and comes on us in a most ferocious way. To illustrate this Lloyd-Jones quoted a little-known hymn by John Newton:

I asked the Lord that I might grow
In faith and love and every grace;
Might more of His salvation know
And seek more earnestly His face.

'Twas He who taught me thus to pray,
And He, I trust, had answered prayer,
But it has been in such a way,
As almost drove me to despair.

I hoped that in some favour'd hour,
At once He'd answer my request,
And by His love's constraining power
Subdue my sins and give me rest.

Instead of this, he made me feel
The hidden evils of my heart,
And let the angry powers of hell
Assault my soul in every part.

Yea more, with His own hand He seemed
Intent to aggravate my woe,
Cross'd all the fair designs I schemed,
Blasted my gourd and laid me low.

Lord, why is this, I trembling cried,
Wilt Thou pursue Thy worm to death?

It is in this way, the Lord replied,
I answer prayer for grace and faith.

These inward trials I employ,
From self and pride to set thee free;
And brake thy schemes of earthly joy,
That thou may'st seek thy all in Me.

Following his dramatic conversion, Newton is here concerned about his sanctification. He prays that God, at a stroke, would deliver him from all sin and that he might enjoy peace. Newton asked the Lord to sanctify him. What happened was that he was shown 'the hidden evils' of his heart. Then hell was let loose on him and he did not know what was happening. Newton asked God to explain this. And the answer came that this was God's way of making people holy – this was sanctification. Lloyd-Jones explains: 'You have to have self crushed out, and it is the only way. The "positive" gospel will not do it, and so you have to have hell let loose, and you will be crushed to the ground.' Newton cries to God for help, and his self has to be smashed before God reveals himself. This is the common experience of all God's most faithful followers. They came to see that this was God's way and that there were no short cuts to sanctification.

SCIENCE
See also **Discoveries**
Speaking of his studies and discoveries, the astronomer Johann Kepler said, 'O God, I am thinking your thoughts after you.'

While orbiting the earth in a space capsule, the astronaut L. Gordon Cooper, Jr., prayed: 'Father, we thank you, especially for letting me fly this flight ... for the privilege of being able to be in this position, to be in this wondrous place, seeing all these many startling, wonderful things that you have created.'

As he neared death, the scientist Michael Faraday said, 'Speculations I have none. I'm resting on certainties. "For I know whom I have believed, and am persuaded that he is able to keep that which I have committed unto him against that day" ' (2 Timothy 1:12).

'What hath God wrought!' (Numbers 23:23 AV). This was Samuel Morse's first message sent by electric telegraph in 1844.

SECOND COMING
See **Jesus Christ**: Jesus' second coming

SELF-PROMOTION
In Westminster Abbey, in the area known as Poets' Corner, lies the memorial to John Milton. Many people have taken a dislike to it. It reads:

> In the year of our Lord Christ
> One thousand seven hundred thirty and seven
> This Bust
> of the author of PARADISE LOST
> was placed there by William Benson Esquire
> One of the two Auditors of the Imprest
> to his Majesty King George the Second
> formerly
> Surveyer General of the Works
> to his majesty King George the First Rysbrack
> Who was the Statuary who cut it ...

One visitor to Poets' Corner who read this said, 'When I first saw this memorial, I had to read it twice. I had to ask myself, "Who is this all about?" Then I understood. It is all about William Benson! He put up the memorial as a device to highlight his own unimportant name, and to become noticed. Milton is merely the excuse!'

Some Christians giving their testimonies seem to be guilty of using William Benson's device. He used the name of the Puritan poet to bring attention to himself. In the same way it is possible to use the name of Jesus Christ, not to point others to him, but to fix their attention on us.

SERVICE
See also **God**: Serving God/Christ
And so, my fellow Americans, ask not what your country can do for you; ask what you can do for your country.
J. F. Kennedy

SIGNS AND WONDERS
See **Miracles**

SIN
A fault confessed is half redressed.
Author unknown

One leak will sink a ship; and one sin will destroy a sinner.
John Bunyan (Pilgrim's Progress)

A fault, once denied, is twice committed.
Thomas Fuller

SOCIAL ACTION
See also **Poverty**

'My brothers and sisters, the evangelical tradition is free salvation, scriptural holiness and social righteousness.' So said John Wesley in a letter to William Wilberforce, encouraging him in his fight against slavery.

Mother Teresa and her Sisters had looked after the sick and dying on the streets of Calcutta for five years. The hospitals were all full up. Eventually Mother Teresa went to Calcutta City Council and spoke to them about the shame of people dying on the streets of the city. The only solution the Calcutta health officer could come up with was a building near the huge Hindu temple. Previously it had been used as a rest room by Hindu worshippers. Now it had fallen into disuse and was only used by drunken tramps and gamblers.

However, Mother Teresa realized that many poor people in the city came to this place as they neared death, since it was regarded as a holy place by the Hindus. To Mother Teresa it didn't matter whether her patients were Sikhs, Buddhists, Muslims or Hindus. All she cared about was showing the love of Jesus to poor, dying people. She believed that she was literally following Jesus' words in the parable of the sheep and the goats: 'Whatever you did for the least of these brothers of mine, you did for me.' She gratefully accepted permission to use the building. Her first patients were being cared for there within a day. The Hindus were very suspicious of her, and some were so hostile that they threw stones at her, hoping to send her packing.

A few days later Mother Teresa saw a crowd collecting just outside the Hindu temple. In the middle of it lay a man in the final stages of cholera. Nobody dared to touch him. To everyone's astonishment, Mother Teresa knelt down next to the man, picked him up herself, and carried him off to her newly acquired home for the dying. There, the man died in peace and dignity. He had been a priest in the Hindu temple. As a result of this event Mother Teresa became accepted and trusted by the Hindus.

In the 1860s the young Thomas Barnardo came from Dublin to London with one Bible verse ringing in his ears: 'Whom shall I send? And who will go for us?' (Isaiah 6:8). Barnardo had made up his mind to become a missionary in China. Because he wanted to care for the whole person – bodies as well as souls – he thought he would become a medical missionary. In the little time he had to spare from his medical training, he met up with some very deprived and poor children in London's East End. At the end of one of these meetings, one boy, Jim Jarvis, refused to leave Barnardo. Barnardo kept on telling him to go home. Jim simply said that he did not have any home to go to. From Jim, Barnardo learned that many young children slept rough in the East End, but he still had his sights firmly set on China.

A few days later Barnardo met Lord Shaftesbury, the Christian philanthropist, at a dinner party. When Barnardo told Shaftesbury about Jim Jarvis, he would not believe the story. Straightaway Barnardo took all the people from the party to a warehouse in Whitechapel. It was full of huge bales covered with tarpaulins, and there were certainly no signs of life. Barnardo knew what to do. He reached between two bales and pulled out a very dirty, dishevelled boy. The boy boasted that he could produce another 20 boys. Within a few minutes, from every corner and hiding-place in the warehouse, 73 boys stood around Lord Shaftesbury.

Not long after this Shaftesbury said to Barnardo, 'Are you sure that it is to China God is sending you?' From that moment Barnardo realized that God was calling him to care for the homeless boys on his own doorstep, rather than the people in far-off China. Seeing the need and suffering around him, Barnardo responded and became the founder of numerous orphanages, which bear his name to this day.

While women weep, as they do now, I'll fight; while men go to prison, in and out, as they do now, I'll fight; while there is a drunkard left, while there is a poor lost girl upon the streets, where there remains one dark soul without the love of God – I'll fight! I'll fight to the very end.

William Booth (from his last speech)

Some Christians once lived in a beautiful village at the foot of a mountain. A road with many dangerous hair-pin bends wound its way up one side of the mountain and down the other side. On these bends there were frequent fatal car accidents. The Christians in this village realized that they had a responsibility to do something about these accidents. They had an all-night prayer meeting and raised enough money, through much sacrificial giving, to buy an ambulance. They organized a 24-hour rota so that the ambulance was available day and night to ferry the injured to the hospital in the next village. Many lives were saved.

A visitor arrived and stayed in the village one day. He heard about the wonderful work the Christians had performed with their voluntary ambulance service. He was totally unimpressed. He began asking awkward, disturbing questions: 'Why don't you close the dangerous roads and build a tunnel?' The Christians were most upset – not because the tunnel idea was not technically feasible, but because the roads had been there for so many years – longer than anyone could remember. Also they were in awe of the mayor. He was the proprietor of two popular restaurants on either side of the mountain. 'You must talk to the mayor,' the troublesome visitor insisted. 'After all, he's a member of your own church!'

Eventually the Christians explained their fundamental objection to such a course of action: 'It's not our place to change the world. Politics is the concern of politicians. We are church members, and our job is to preach the Gospel. The Gospel must not become involved in political issues.'

Before he left the beautiful village the visitor asked the Christians: 'Do you want to be ambulance drivers or tunnel builders? Are you being more spiritual by picking up gory bodies after accidents – victims of destructive social structures – or should you be bending all your energies into changing those evil structures?'

In 1983, when he was 11 years old, Trevor Farrel saw a television programme about the plight of homeless people in Philadelphia, about 18 miles from his home. He persuaded his parents to drive there with a blanket and a pillow to give to a homeless person. Each night after that they drove into the city, until they had nothing left to give away.

Then Trevor advertised the needs of the homeless in Philadelphia and asked for gifts of old blankets, pillows and warm clothes. His story was taken up by a television station and a newspaper. So many gifts came in that a warehouse had to be found to hold everything. A church gave a shelter with 33 rooms, which they called 'Trevor's Place'. Within two years 250 people were joining Trevor and his parents each night to serve hot meals to the homeless.

SOWING AND REAPING

Sow a thought, reap a word;
sow a word, reap a deed;
sow a deed, reap a habit;
sow a habit, reap a character;
sow a character, reap a destiny.
Author unknown

STARTING

See also **Procrastination**
A journey of a thousand miles must begin with a single step.
Lao Tzu (Chinese philosopher)

He who deliberates fully before taking a step will spend his entire life on one leg.
Chinese proverb

STEWARDSHIP

See **Giving to God**

STUDY

Billy Graham was once asked if he had any regrets about the way he had spent his life as an evangelist, and how he would have used his time differently if he could live his life again. He replied, 'One of my great regrets is that I have not studied enough. I wish I had studied more and preached less.' He went on to explain that sometimes he had accepted invitations to speak to different groups of people when he knew that he needed to spend more time in study.

Donald Barnhouse once said, 'If I knew that the Lord was coming back in three years time, I would spend two years studying, and only one year in preaching.'

SUCCESS

The figure of the Crucified invalidates all thought which takes success for its standard.
Dietrich Bonhoeffer

Robert Redford, who stole hubcaps in high school and lost his college baseball scholarship through drunkenness, became America's most popular movie actor in the mid–1970s for his roles in *The Way We Were* and *The Sting*. Redford used his influence to advance environmental causes, and he used his money to establish the Sundance Institute for aspiring film-makers. Its annual film festival has become one of the world's most influential.

Norma Jean Mortenson (later known to the world as Marilyn Monroe) was born on 1 June 1926 in Los Angeles General Hospital. Her mother, Gladys, listed the father's address as 'unknown'. Norma Jean would never know the true identity of her father.

Due to her mother's mental instability and the fact that she was unmarried at the time, Norma Jean was placed with foster-parents, Albert and Ida Bolender, with whom she lived the first seven years of her life. She once said of the Bolenders, 'They were terribly strict... They didn't mean any harm... It was their religion. They brought me up harshly.'

Norma Jean lived in an orphanage from 1935 to 1937. She recalled, 'The world around me then was kind of grim. I had to learn to pretend in order to ... block the grimness. The whole world seemed sort of closed to me ... I felt on the outside of everything, and all I could do was to dream up any kind of pretend-game.'

In June 1942 Norma Jean married Jim Dougherty. She later said, 'My foster mother Grace McKee arranged the marriage for me. I never had a choice. There's not much to say about it. They couldn't support me, and they had to work out something. And so I got married.'

In July 1946 she signed a contract with Twentieth Century Fox Studios. She chose her mother's family name of Monroe. From this point on she would be known as Marilyn Monroe to all her fans.

In the autumn of 1946 she was granted a divorce. Later she said, 'My marriage didn't make me sad, but it didn't make me happy either. My husband and I hardly spoke to each other. This wasn't because we were angry. We had nothing to say. I was dying of boredom.'

Despite enormous popular success in a series of comedy films such as *The Seven Year Itch* (1955) and *The Prince and the Showgirl* (1955), and despite becoming the sex symbol of the 1950s, Marilyn Monroe committed suicide in 1962.

Each of the five young women who make up the Spice Girls (their nicknames are Ginger Spice, Baby Spice, Posh Spice, Scary Spice and Sporty Spice) is expected to make over £3 million in 1997. They can claim to be the most successful British pop group of all time, in that their first single *Wannabe* was the best-selling first record release of all time in the British charts. It was No. 1 in the US charts within four weeks of being released, which no other British group has ever managed with its first release. Their first four singles all went to the No. 1 spot in the British charts, which no other group – not even the Beatles – has ever managed.

Michael Jackson, the star, is a phenomenon. From the way he moves, to the Neverland he's created at his home, it's as if he is an illusion.
Stephen Spielberg

SUFFERING
See also **Torture; Tragedy**
George Matheson (1842–1906), the son of a Glasgow merchant, practically lost his eyesight when he was 18. He was outstanding in his studies at Edinburgh University. In 1868 he became the parish minister at Inellan, and in 1886 the minister at St Bernard's Edinburgh. His famous hymn 'O Love, that will not let me go' was written in the manse at Inellan on the evening of 6 June 1882, just after his fiancée had called off their engagement because of his blindness. Matheson wrote:

I was at that time alone. It was the day of my sister's marriage, and the rest of the family were staying overnight in Glasgow. Something happened to me which was known only to myself, and which caused me the most severe mental suffering. The hymn was the fruit of that suffering. It was the quickest bit of work I ever did in my life. I had the impression rather of having it dictated to me by some inward voice than of working it out myself. I am quite sure that the whole work was completed in five minutes, and equally sure it never received at my hands any retouching or correction.

> O Love, that wilt not let me go,
> I rest my weary soul in Thee;
> I give Thee back the life I owe,
> That in Thine ocean depths its flow
> May richer, fuller be.
>
> O Light, that followest all my way,
> I yield my flickering torch to Thee;
> My heart restores its borrowed ray,

That in Thy sunshine's blaze its day
May brighter, fairer be.

O Joy, that seekest me through pain,
I cannot close my heart to Thee;
I trace the rainbow through the rain,
And feel the promise is not vain
That morn shall tearless be.

O Cross, that liftest up my head,
I dare not ask to fly from Thee;
I lay in dust life's glory dead,
And from the ground there blossoms red
Life that shall endless be.

Later on, sensing the meaning behind his suffering, Matheson wrote:

My God, I have never thanked thee for my thorn. I have been looking forward to a world where I shall get compensated for my cross – but I have never thought of my cross as itself a present glory. Teach me the glory of my cross. Teach me the value of my thorn. Show me that my tears made my rainbow.

Brian Keenan, for four-and-a-half years a hostage in Beirut, endured torture and long periods of solitary confinement. Speaking to an Anglican charity, he said that the importance of 'discovering oneself through solitude' must not be lost. It is when one is alone that one becomes aware of one's 'deepest needs, feelings and desires'. He quoted Alexander Solzhenitsyn, who found that in the greatest suffering there was also a sense of freedom and 'moments of utter happiness'.
Church Times

SUNDAY

Do not let Sunday be taken from you ... If your soul has no Sunday, it becomes an orphan.
Albert Schweitzer

TALENTS

Just before he went abroad, a merchant gave two of his friends two sacks of grain each to take care of until he returned. After a few years he came back and asked for his grain. The first friend took him to his warehouse and showed him the original two sacks, which were now covered in mould and worthless. The second friend took the merchant into the country and showed him fields of grain growing and ripening – the produce of the two sacks which he had used as seed. 'Give me the two sacks,' said the merchant, 'and keep the rest.'

Eastern allegory

A mouse ran over the body of a sleeping lion. The lion woke up, caught the mouse and thought he would eat it. But the mouse begged that he might be spared and said that he would one day pay the lion back for his kindness if he let him go. The lion laughed and released him.

Quite soon after this the lion was caught by hunters and was bound by a rope to a tree. The mouse heard the lion groaning. He ran to him and gnawed through the rope until the lion was free. 'You laughed at me the other day,' said the mouse, 'because you never thought that I would be able to repay your kindness. Now you know that even mice are grateful.'

One of Aesop's fables

TEARS

Men cry on average between 2 and 10 times a year. Women cry an average of 9 to 30 times a year.

Daily Mail

The actress Audrey Hepburn had a problem during the making of the big movie *Roman Holiday:* she couldn't cry on cue. As they were filming the final scene, in which she said farewell to Gregory Peck, she was unable to produce any tears. She refused to let the director, William Wyler, put artificial tears on her cheek. It got later and later. Everyone on the set was exhausted and wanted to go home. But Audrey wouldn't give up.

Finally Wyler blew his top: 'What do you think you're doing?' he shouted. 'You're not professional at all!'

Audrey suddenly burst into a flood of very real tears. Wyler signalled the cameraman, and they captured the moment on film. It was perfect.

An uncomfortable minute passed. No one knew what to say. Wyler walked over to Audrey and gave her a great big hug. All was forgiven.

Audrey won an Oscar for being that year's Best Actress.

TELEVISION

'No other family was as obsessed with TV in my neighbourhood as mine was. We were allowed to watch TV 24 hours a day. And we did. I would literally run home from school every day and switch on my favourite shows.' So wrote Rosie O'Donnell, who in 1997 had a $4 million contract for her hit TV series and a $3 million book deal with Warner Books for her memoirs.

Robson Green, who plays Private Tucker in the British TV series *Soldier, Soldier* and who has starred in the films *Touching Evil* and *Reckless*, has said, 'There's too much violence on TV. Morality has gone out of the window.'

The TV addict's version of Psalm 23:
    The TV is my shepherd, my spiritual life shall want.
    It makes me to sit down and do nothing for the cause of Christ.
    It demandeth my spare time.
    It restoreth my desire for the things of the world.
    It keepeth me from studying the truth of God's Word.
    It leadeth me in the path of failure to attend God's house.
    Yea, though I live to be a hundred, I will fear no rental.
    My 'Telly' is with me, its sound and vision comfort me.
    It prepareth a programme for me, even in the presence of visitors.
    Its volume shall be full.
    Surely comedy and commercials shall follow me all the days of my life,
    And I will dwell in spiritual poverty forever.
Author unknown

TEMPER

While Leonardo da Vinci was working on his great masterpiece, *The Lord's Supper*, he lost his temper with someone and said many unkind things to him. Then he returned to his work. He was painting the face of Jesus, but found that he could not continue with it. Eventually he put his paintbrushes down, went and found the man he had lost his temper with, and asked his forgiveness. After that, da Vinci managed to carry on with his painting.

TEMPTATION

The best way to drive out the devil, if he will not yield to texts of scripture, is to jeer and flout him, for he cannot stand scorn.
Martin Luther

The great Early Church scholar Jerome at one time lived alone as a hermit in the desert, but he had to admit in the end that he could not banish the dark passions which were always at hand to haunt his mind. He later wrote:

How often, when I was living in the desert, parched by a burning sun, did I fancy myself among the pleasures of Rome! Sackcloth disfigured my unshapely limbs, and my skin from long neglect had become as black as an Ethiopian's. And although in my fear of hell I had consigned myself to this prison, where I had no companions but scorpions and wild beasts, I often thought myself in the company of many girls. My face grew pale, and my frame chilled with fasting; yet my mind was burning with desire, and the fires of lust kept bubbling up before me when my flesh was as good as dead. Helpless, I cast myself at the feet of Jesus.

Whenever I'm caught between two evils I take the one I have not yet experienced.
Mae West

THEOLOGY

'There is only one theology, but there are many theologians.' So said Athenagoras I, the Ecumenical Patriarch of Constantinople, when he met the Pope on 5 January 1964. This was the first meeting between a leader of the Greek Orthodox Church and a Pope since 1439.

TIME

On a sundial in a garden close to Gloucester Cathedral is this inscription:

Give God thy heart, thy service and thy gold;
The day wears on and time is waxing old.

Time is always an eternity when you are a child.
Dennis Potter (English playwright)

TORTURE

Leonard Wilson, who later became Bishop of Birmingham, was tortured by the Japanese during World War II. When the Japanese asked him why, since he believed in God, God did not save him, he answered: 'God doesn't save people from punishment or pain. He saves them by giving them the strength and the spirit to bear it.' Later he went back to Japan to baptize one of his torturers, who had come to share Bishop Wilson's faith in Christ because of the way Christ had strengthened him through suffering.

TRAGEDY

Joseph Scriven's life was filled with trouble. He was born in Dublin in 1820 and went to Trinity College there. He emigrated to Canada when he was 25, where he became engaged to a beautiful Christian girl. Together they planned how they would live in their future home, agreeing that everything should be brought to the Lord in prayer, so that their home might be everything that a Christian home should be. The day of the wedding had been arranged, and all the preparations were complete. But the day before the wedding the bride was accidentally drowned.

Scriven was devastated. Then he recalled the agreement that he and his fiancée had made, to take everything to the Lord in prayer together. So Scriven prayed, asking the Lord to give him strength to bear his great loss. After a three-hour-long struggle, peace came to his soul, and he was able to say, 'Thy will be done.'

He became a servant of the underprivileged, helping those who were physically handicapped and financially destitute. But tragedy continued to stalk his steps. Once again, his plans for a wedding were cut short when his second fiancée also died, following a brief illness. It seemed that Scriven was meant to go through life alone, knowing only the friendship of Jesus Christ. For most of his life he experienced loneliness, meagre pay for menial work and much ill health.

Soon after the death of his second fiancée Scriven's mother passed through a debilitating illness. To comfort her Scriven wrote her a hymn, 'What a Friend we have in Jesus'. In Scriven's own last illness a neighbour came to visit him, and the manuscript of this hymn was next to his bed. The neighbour was much impressed by it and asked Scriven if he had written it. Scriven replied, 'The Lord and I did it between us.' The hymn has become famous all over the world.

TRANSFORMATION
See also **Regeneration**
Nature forms us, sin deforms us, school informs us, Christ transforms us.
Author unknown

TREASURE
In October 1966 *The Week* reported that Dr Frank Kermode, a literary critic, had lost 2,500 'priceless books and documents'. He had given his books to some dustmen, thinking that they were removal men!

TREES
Through a tree we were made debtors to God; so through a tree we have our debt cancelled.
Irenaeus of Lyons

TRINITY
Without the Spirit it is not possible to hold the Word of God nor without the Son can any draw near to the Father, for the knowledge of the Father is the Son and the knowledge of the Son of God is through the Holy Spirit.
Irenaeus of Lyons

TRUSTING GOD
By a mathematical coincidence, the central verse in the Bible is Psalm 118:8: 'It is better to take refuge in the Lord than to trust in man.' This focuses our attention on the fact that trusting God is one of the fundamental principles of the Bible.

The God we serve is mighty indeed and I will never forget who it is who gives me my strength.
Jonathan Edwards (world triple jump record holder)

All will be well, and all will be well, and all manner of things will be well.
Julian of Norwich (Revelations of Divine Love)

In his Journal for 13 May 1872 David Livingstone the explorer wrote: 'He will keep His word – the gracious One, full of grace and truth; no doubt of it. He said, "Him that cometh unto Me, I will in no wise cast out"; and "Whatsoever ye shall ask in My name, I will give it." He will keep his word; then I can come and humbly present my petition and it will be all right. Doubt is here inadmissible, surely.'

I have two planks for a bed, two stools, two cups and a basin. On my broken wall is a small card which says, 'God hath chosen the weak things – I can do all things through Christ who strengthens me.' It is true I have passed through fire.
Gladys Aylward

Let nothing disturb you,
nothing frighten you;
All things are passing;
God never changes;
Patient endurance
Attains all things;
Whoever possesses God
Lacks nothing;
God alone suffices.
Teresa of Avila

Mary Slessor (1848–1915) worked for 16 years in the mills of Dundee to earn enough money for her family. She is remembered for her pioneer missionary work in West Africa. She gave herself in tireless service for the sick, in educating children, and in opposing local customs such as child sacrifice and the killing of twins at birth. In her Bible next to Psalm 3:6 she wrote seven words which became her motto: 'God and one are always a majority.'

Trust the past to God's mercy,
the present to his love,
and the future to his providence.
Augustine

TRUTH

An anagram of the Latin phrase *Quid est veritas?* ('What is truth?') is *Est Vir qui adest* ('It is the Man who is before thee').

When Sir Robert Armstrong, the British Cabinet Secretary, was being cross-examined in the Supreme Court of New South Wales in November 1986 during the famous controversy surrounding Peter Wright's book *Spycatcher*, he said, 'As one person said, "I have been economical with the truth." ' The person he was quoting was Edmund Burke.

TWENTIETH CENTURY

I consider the greatest dangers of the twentieth century to be:
1. Religion without the Holy Ghost.
2. Christianity without Christ.
3. Forgiveness without regeneration.
4. Morality without God.
5. Heaven without hell.
General William Booth

UNITY

As a young man, Brother Roger was amazed that Christians spent so long justifying their differences. He felt that the most powerful way to reveal Christ in the world would be to create a community in which people gave their lives to bring about reconciliation in practical ways in everyday living.

In the summer of 1940, not long after the start of World War II, when he was 25, Brother Roger felt that the time had come. He set off into France on his bike, looking for a house where he could pray, and where others could be welcomed.

He arrived at Taizé. There was no road, only a track. There was no telephone, no running water, no parish priest. He writes: 'I was struck by the warm-hearted welcome of a few elderly people. One of them invited me for a meal and suggested: "Stay here. We are so lonely, and the winters are so long." '

That was the beginning of the Taizé community. Today thousands of people go there every year. There are also some small Taizé communities in poor neighbourhoods in Asia, Africa, North America and South America.

This was the motto of Richard Baxter, a seventeenth-century English Puritan preacher:

In necessary things, unity;
in doubtful things, liberty;
in all things, charity.

Above all, do not divide into sects and groups, each quarrelling with the others. When we are split into sects our attenion is drawn away from inward grace to outward works, each sect trying to rove it is better than the other. Sects arise when people wrongly set themselves up as presbyters and prophets, winning allegiance not by the truth of their teaching but by their charm. Such people will always be present, ready to foster dissension, and it is for all of us to discern their falsehood and guard against them.

Martin Luther

A farmer's sons were always arguing. He tried to stop them, but without success. So he decided to give them an object lesson. He told them to bring him a bundle of sticks. Then he gave the bundle to each of his sons in turn, asking them to break the sticks. No matter how hard they tried, they failed. Then the farmer untied the bundle and handed the sticks out, one at a time, to his sons. Then they had no trouble in breaking the sticks.

'It's the same with you, my sons,' the farmer said. 'So long as you agree together, no enemy can defeat you. But if you quarrel you will become an easy prey.'

Moral: Divided, men are vulnerable; they are made strong when they are united.

One of Aesop's fables

Tous pour un, un pour tous ('All for one and one for all'). This is the famous motto of the three heroes in Alexandre Dumas' novel *The Three Musketeers*.

John Winthrop, from Suffolk, England, explained his vision of government in the New World as he sailed in the *Arabella* across the Atlantic to New England. This section of his sermon is chiselled in stone on Boston Common. Presidents Kennedy and Reagan both frequently quoted from it:

The only way to avoid shipwreck and to provide for our prosperity, is to follow the counsel of Micah, to do justly, to love mercy and to walk humbly with our God. For this end, we must be knit together, in this work, as one man. We must entertain each other in brotherly affection. We must be willing to abridge ourselves of our superfluities, for the supply of others' necessities. We must uphold a familiar commerce together in all meekness, gentleness, patience, and liberality.

We must delight in each other; make others' condition our own; rejoice together, mourn together, labour and suffer together, always having before our eyes our commission and community in the work, as members of the same body. So shall we keep the unity of the spirit in the bond of peace. The Lord will be our God, and delight to dwell among us, as his own people, and will command a blessing upon us in all our ways. So that we shall see much more of his wisdom, power, goodness and truth, than formerly we have been acquainted with. We shall find that the God of Israel is among us, when ten of us shall be able to resist a thousand of our enemies; when he shall make us a praise and a glory, that men shall say of succeeding plantations, 'The Lord make it like that of New England.' For we must consider that we shall be as a city upon a hill. The eyes of all people are upon us.

VISIONS

I went back to the forest to pray, after I had finished my work. As I sat on a rock I thought about what blessings to pray for. While I was doing this it seemed as though another person came and stood near me. From his bearing and dress and way of speaking, he seemed to me to be a well respected and devoted servant of God, yet his eyes glittered with deceit and cunning. As he spoke it was as if he breathed an odour of hell. He said to me:

'Holy and honoured sir, pardon me for interrupting your prayers and breaking in on your privacy. But it is one's duty to try to promote the welfare of others, so I have come to lay an important matter before you. Your pure unselfish life has made a deep impression not only on me but on a great number of devout people. In God's name you have sacrificed yourself body and soul for others, but have you been truly appreciated? What I mean is, as a Christian you have influenced only a few thousand other Christians, some of whom even distrust you. Wouldn't it be much more worth while if you became a Hindu or a Muslim? Then you could really become a great leader. They are looking for such a spiritual leader. Consider what I'm suggesting; if you accept it, then three hundred and ten million Hindus and Muslims will become your followers. And pay you enormous respect and honour.'

As soon as I heard this, these words rushed from my lips: 'You Satan! Get out! I knew you immediately. You're the wolf in sheep's clothes! Your single desire is for me to renounce the cross and the narrow path that leads to life, and to choose the broad road of death. My Master himself is my lot and my life. He gave himself, his very life, for me and so it is right that I should offer my own life to him as a sacrifice, for he is everything to me. Get away! I have nothing to do with you.'

On hearing my reply the deceiver went off grumbling and growling in rage. I, in my tears, poured out my soul to God in prayer. 'My Lord God, you who are everything to me, life of my life, spirit of my spirit, look on me in mercy, so fill me with your Spirit that my heart shall have no room for love of anything else but you alone. Amen.'

When I rose from this prayer I half-saw through my tears, a glowing being dressed in light and beauty, standing before me. Though he did not speak a word yet there poured from him lightning-like rays of life-giving love, the·power of which penetrated and bathed my very soul. At once I knew that my dear Saviour stood before me. Immediately I arose from my

seat upon the rock and fell at his feet. He held in his hand the key of my heart. Opening its innermost chamber with his key of love, he filled me with his presence, and whenever I looked within or outside myself I saw only him.
Sundar Singh

VOCATION

Many people mistake our work for our vocation. Our vocation is the love of Jesus.
Mother Teresa

WILL OF GOD
See **God:** The will of God

WISDOM
Some things worth remembering:

The value of time.
The success of perseverance.
The pleasure of working.
The dignity of simplicity.
The worth of character.
The improvement of talent.
The influence of example.
The obligation of duty.
The wisdom of economy.
The virtue of patience.
The joy of originating.
The power of darkness.
Author unknown

WITNESS, WITNESSING
See also **Martyrdom; Persecution**
Michael Caine, the actor, was born a Cockney. His father was a porter at Billingsgate fish-market in the East End of London, and his mother was a cleaner. In an interview in *The Guardian* he said, 'I was taken off the streets by a guy called Reverend Butterworth', who ran an amateur dramatics society at a local youth club.
The Week

I believe God is primarily calling me to be a witness where I am … rather than a celebrity Christian speaking at a different church each Sunday.
Kriss Akabusi

William Wilberforce did more than any other person to rid the British Empire of slavery. In Parliament, where he had a reputation as a very eloquent speaker, he was known as 'the Nightingale of the House of Commons', and MPs always crowded in to hear him whenever he spoke.

On his death they arranged for a tomb to be erected in his honour in Westminster Abbey. However, nothing on the tombstone referred to his eloquent speeches. Instead they had these words inscribed: 'The abiding eloquence of a Christian life.' To his friends the unseen influence of Wilberforce's Christian life was more powerful than any eloquent speech.

When Henry Stanley went out to Africa in 1871 and found David Livingstone, he spent some months in Livingstone's company, but the great missionary-explorer never spoke to him directly about his faith in Christ. Throughout these months Stanley watched the old man. He could not understand Livingstone's daily routine, and he had never met another man who exhibited such patience. Stanley never understood Livingstone's sympathy for the Africans. For the sake of Christ and the Gospel, he showed endless patience as his own health constantly declined. Stanley wrote: 'When I saw the unwearied patience, that unflagging zeal, those enlightened sons of Africa, I became a Christian at his side, though he never spoke to me about it.'

WOMEN

In 1919 Nancy Witcher Langhorne Astor (1879–1946) became the very first female MP in the British House of Commons. She supported the campaign for women's rights and the temperance movement.

Emily Wilding Davison (1872–1913), an English suffragette, tried to grab the reins of the racehorse owned by the king near the end of the 1913 Derby race. She died from her injuries a few days later.

Elizabeth Garrett Anderson (1836–1917) was the first woman doctor allowed to practice in England. Against great prejudice from male doctors, she passed her medical examinations in 1865 and worked in the East London Hospital. In 1874 she founded the London School of Medicine for Women. She became the first woman mayor in England when she was elected mayor of her home town, Aldeburgh in Suffolk.

Why have women passion, intellect, moral activity – these three – and a place in society where no one of these three can be exercised?
Florence Nightingale

I myself have never been able to find out precisely what feminism is; I only know that people call me a feminist whenever I express sentiments that differentiate me from a doormat.
Rebecca West (twentieth-century author)

WORK
See also **Dedication; Vocation**
Extreme busyness, whether at school or college, kirk or market, is a symptom of deficient vitality.
Robert Louis Stevenson

'Thank God, I was born poor. I learned how to work.' So said Del Smith, the millionaire founder and chairman of Evergreen International Aviation.

Without God, we cannot. Without us, God will not.
Augustine

Thomas Edison (1847–1931) was a tireless inventor who patented over 1,000 inventions during his lifetime, including the electrical voice recorder (1869); the automatic repeating telegraph (1870); the printing telegraph (1871); the phonograph (1877); the light bulb (1879); and the first hydro-electric power station (1882). According to Edison, genius is 'one per cent inspiration and ninety-nine per cent perspiration.'

I tried on 250 bathing suits in one afternoon and ended up having little scabs up and down my thighs, probably from some of those with sequins all over them.
Cindy Crawford (supermodel)

WORKAHOLISM
With more and more church leaders becoming victims of heart attacks, the Coronary Club is extending membership to those who only a few

years ago were considered much too young to be admitted. The following rules, if followed, will assure speedy action toward membership:

1. Never say No.
2. Insist on being liked by, and trying to please, everyone.
3. Never delegate responsibility. If you must appoint a committee, do all the work yourself.
4. Never plan a day off, but if you are forced to take one, visit a preacher friend and spend the day talking about church problems, yours and his.
5. Never allow enough time to drive comfortably to an appointment. (This will do two things: show people how busy you are; protect the reputation preachers have as fast drivers.)
6. When the doctor advises you to slow down, ignore him and brag about the fact that you would rather wear out than rust out.
7. Lead your church into a building programme whether they need it or not; consider yourself better qualified than the architect and give it your personal supervision.
8. Consider it your civic duty to be a member of every club in town and become president of as many as you can.
9. If having done all these, you don't succeed, accept the largest church you can find and work tirelessly.

Author unknown

WORLD, END OF THE

In January 1997 a meteor landed in Honduras, leaving blazing coffee fields and a 165-feet-deep crater. If the meteor had struck 10 hours earlier it would have destroyed Bangkok… In 1989 our planet missed a collision with a 500-metre-wide asteroid by a mere six hours… There are already 200 craters on the earth, left by small asteroids.

The Week

According to scientists, 65 million years ago an asteroid 10 kilometres wide crashed into the Earth, resulting in the destruction of the dinosaurs and nine tenths of all life on the earth.

WORRY

Tomorrow has two handles: the handle of fear and the handle of faith. You can take hold of it by either handle.

Author unknown

In all trouble you should seek God. You should not set him over against your troubles, but within them. God can only relieve your troubles if you in your anxiety cling to him. Trouble should not really be thought of as this thing or that in particular, for our whole life on earth involves trouble; and through the troubles of our earthly pilgrimage we find God.
Augustine

Anxiety does not empty tomorrow of its sorrows, but only empties today of its strength.
C. H. Spurgeon

Anxiety is the greatest evil that can befall us except sin; for just as revolt and sedition in a country cause havoc and sap its resistance to a foreign invasion, so we, when troubled and worried, are unable to preserve the virtues we have already acquired, or resist the temptations of the devil, who then diligently fishes, as they say, in troubled waters.
Francis de Sales

Good morning, theologians! You wake and sing. But I, old fool, know less than you and worry over everything, instead of simply trusting in the heavenly Father's care.
Martin Luther (talking to the birds as he walked through the woods)

WORSHIP
'Sing to the Lord a new song,' the psalm tells us. 'I do sing!' you may reply. You sing, of course you sing. I can hear you. But make sure that your life sings the same tune as your mouth. Sing with your voices. Sing with your hearts. Sing with your lips. Sing with your lives. Be yourselves what the words are about! If you live good lives, you yourselves are the songs of new life.
Augustine

WRITING
The author would wish his work to be brought to this test – does it uniformly tend

To humble the sinner?
To exalt the Saviour?
To promote holiness?

If in any one instance it loses sight of any of these points, let it be condemned without mercy.
Charles Simeon